Coaching a Season of Significance

COACHING

a season of

SIGNIFICANCE

A Soccer Coaches' Companion to All Challenges of a Year

GREG WINKLER

Meyer & Meyer Sport

British Library Cataloguing in Publication Data
A catalogue record for this book is available from the British Library

Coaching a Season of Significance
Maidenhead: Meyer & Meyer Sport (UK) Ltd., 2017
ISBN: 978-1-78255-106-5

© 2017 by Meyer & Meyer Sport (UK) Ltd.
Aachen, Auckland, Beirut, Cairo, Cape Town, Dubai, Hägendorf, Hong Kong, Indianapolis, Manila, New Delhi, Singapore, Sydney, Tehran, Vienna
 Member of the World Sport Publishers' Association (WSPA)
Printed & Binded: Color House Graphics, Grand Rapids, MI, USA
E-Mail: info@m-m-sports.com
www.m-m-sports.com

TABLE OF CONTENTS

1 PREFACE

Coaching and teaching have been passions of mine my entire life. I grew up playing the traditional sports in high school, gravitating towards football, wrestling, and track and then spending many years afterwards coaching those sports. It wasn't until later in my coaching career that I found soccer—or rather, soccer found me.

It was April of 1989 when I received a phone call from a desperate parent, begging me to coach my six-year-old son, Bart, and his recreational soccer team. At the time I was teaching elementary physical education and served as an assistant coach for the high school football, wrestling, and track teams. These were all sports I grew up playing and I felt confident sharing my knowledge of those activities with young athletes.

Soccer, on the other hand, was not offered when I was in high school and my knowledge of the game—much like the sport's popularity in the United States—was minimal at best.

I politely told the panicked parent that I would help someone coach my son's team, but I simply did not know enough about soccer to take on a team by myself.

Since co-coaching and eventually taking over my son's team in the summer of '89, I haven't looked back. I coached young Bart's team every season until he entered high school and did the same with our three sons after him. In the fall of 1998, I became the head coach of the Fond du Lac High School varsity boys' soccer team, and eventually took on the same duties with the girl's varsity team in 2006. My coaching and life journey took me to the state of Florida in 2014, where I took over the George Jenkins girls' program in Lakeland before landing in Cape Coral at Ida Baker High School in 2015, coaching the boys' team.

Over 35 years of coaching and more than 75 soccer teams later, I still cannot believe my initial reluctance toward coaching soccer to a bunch of six-year-olds.

It's impossible to coach for close to four decades—and survive—without learning how to teach young athletes to handle themselves in triumph and adversity. Coaching is more than just throwing out the ball and filling out a lineup, and as the years went by it became more and more clear to me that wins and losses alone do not determine the success of each particular team. Regardless of the talent or the age group, I realized that my goal as a coach is to ensure that each season is a season of significance for all the athletes involved.

As my knowledge of soccer and the coaching profession increased, so too did my thirst for more knowledge on both topics. To quench that thirst, I devoured the coaching biographies of Lou Holtz, Anson Dorrance, John Wooden, and Pete Carroll, among others, along with training manuals and books about coaching techniques, team building, and mental training. If there's a book about coaching, I've more than likely read it.

Yet through my reading, I hadn't come across a comprehensive book on how to have success in youth and high school athletics both on and off the field. Since I found myself answering some of the same questions from other coaches and parents over and over again, I decided to put together a coaching guide of my own, which turned into this book. Hopefully, from my experiences of co-coaching that first soccer team to taking over the program at one of the largest high schools in Wisconsin, this book will help you build a foundation for your own program.

All told, I've been on the sidelines of a football field, basketball court, wrestling mat, track and, of course, the soccer pitch. While the bulk of my experiences come from coaching soccer, the information provided throughout the following pages is transferable to all sports.

Whether you're already a coach and looking for ways to make your program stand out or a young father fielding a call from a desperate soccer club, this book should serve as a guideline on how to run a high school or youth sports team, with an emphasis on leadership, communication, and building relationships. Coaching soccer has been my avenue to practice and refine these skills. Whatever your sport is, it is time to make every season a season of significance.

2 INTRODUCTION

Each and every one of us has personal goals for ourselves, our families, our careers, and for the teams we coach. My goal for every team I coach is for each season to be a significant one, so memorable that every player will treasure and remember the experience throughout their lifetime. So what are the characteristics of a significant season?

There are three key elements needed for a season to be remembered and for that season to have a lasting impression on your team.

1. **The season needs to be meaningful.** Did the players take something away from it at season's end? Did they improve their individual skills or understanding of the game? Did they master a new team tactic? Was a meaningful relationship formed or enhanced between you, the coach, and the team? If you can answer yes to any of those questions, you more than likely satisfied element number one.

2. **The season needs to be important.** Did you make the season important to the players? A season can be important for many of the same reasons that it was meaningful. If the season wasn't important to an individual player, how valuable was that player to your team? Each player needs to feel involved in the team goals. If they do not feel like a part of the process, regardless of his or her respective role within the team, was it really important to them? For the season to be important, the team has to believe in the goals and overall mission that either the coach has put before them or that they have decided on together.

3. **The season needs to be memorable.** Was the season memorable in the eyes of the players? It could be memorable because the team won a conference or district title, or had a winning record for the first time, or beat a long-time rival. Achievements and milestones make the season memorable. But what if those accolades don't come? Can you still have a memorable season? The answer is of course, yes.

For example, you may be taking on the challenge of creating a program from scratch. Or you could be in the developmental years of your program, still trying to grow and gain recognition. Or your club lacks character, direction, or confidence and is in need of a culture change. Or, after enjoying some success, your team is taking on a more challenging schedule. In these cases, progress made toward shaping or improving upon your program may be greatly rewarding to you and your players. While winning is definitely a goal to be achieved, it is not always a necessary factor for a significant season.

2.1 PHILOSOPHY

In order to obtain that significant season, you need something to guide you in your decision making process. What are you about and what do you want your program to represent? I remember interviewing for a junior high teaching position that included head football, wrestling, and track coaching duties. The principal, Michael Nault, asked me one seemingly simple question: "What is your philosophy of coaching?"

As an aspiring young coach I had researched the school and spoken to other coaches and teachers in the district, and I came to find out that while Mr. Nault believed in opportunities and participation at the junior high level, he was also very competitive. I gave a lengthy and detailed response, covering everything that I believed. He was satisfied with my stated desire to lead a successful and winning program, but without sacrificing the opportunity for young athletes to compete and test their skills in competition.

Over the years, as I gained experience dealing with young athletes, parents, and administrative figures, my philosophy has matured and become much easier to explain, no longer requiring the lengthy explanation I gave Mr. Nault. Longtime football coach Pete Carroll titled his book, *Always Compete*, which summarizes his own philosophy and explains how easy it is to apply. As I thought about his simple mantra, I thought about my own message to my teams and found a philosophy that fits what I do every day.

If I had that same interview with Mr. Nault now, I would tell him that my philosophy is to make a difference. When I speak to my teams or talk to parents, or I interview for positions, I make it clear that my goal is simply to make a difference, be it on the field, in the classroom, in the community, or within my family.

If you do not have a coaching philosophy, take a moment to reflect on why you are coaching and what you personally want out of it as well as what you want your teams to reflect. At the same time, make sure it is a reasonable goal; you have to be able to walk the talk, so you want to make sure your philosophy is something that you can represent.

2.2 COACHING RULES

For new coaches, or for those embarking upon a new job or relationship, here are twelve rules to follow as you begin your journey:

1. Have an attitude of gratitude.

2. Be humble.

3. Set expectations.

4. Celebrate the positives.

5. Listen to your team and empower your captains.

6. Continue to educate yourself.

7. Integrity is number one!

8. Teach and model respect and sportsmanship.

9. Embrace the past by valuing team traditions.

10. Build relationships.

11. Communicate, communicate, communicate!

12. Have FUN and enjoy the ride!

3 PUTTING CHARACTER FIRST

When I started coaching, my biggest worries were about our formation and tactics, how I would organize my practice session, and whether or not the players would listen to me. The idea of teaching character was not even on the radar.

When I took over as a high school coach, I had it all figured out. My team rules were in place and I had athletic players that came from good families. The last thing I was worried about was character development; I just wanted to train them hard and win some games. We had better success on the field than the program was accustomed to and we had more talented players with each passing year. Soccer was growing in the community, and as the high school varsity coach, I was reaping the rewards of that growth. Five years into the program, my team reached the sectional finals for the second time since I took over the program.

But despite the talented team on the field, I soon found out that we had some serious character issues off the field.

I had heard some troubling rumors about off-field behavior, but there was no evidence of any problems and the team was performing on the field. Who was I to question a rumor and possibly rock the boat? Then in one moment, our lack of team character was exposed. We were playing a more talented team that had beaten us during the regular season through their physicality and gamesmanship (along with some expert floppers on the squad prepared to embellish any contact and influence the referee).

We had a solid game plan entering the contest, but a questionable call in the penalty box resulted in a penalty kick and a 1-0 deficit that would change the way I viewed my coaching curriculum. Our team continued to play hard but we did not handle the adversity well and lost our composure as well as the game. My frustration with the tactics of the opposing coach and my own team's lack of character led to a verbal clash after the contest between my players and the opponents. My goalkeeper, when presented with the runner-up medal, used his great distribution ability and tossed his medal out of the stadium and into the street. We represented ourselves poorly and as the coach I was responsible for the display of bad sportsmanship. It was not the kind of behavior I expected of my teams.

Months after the season ended, another issue revealed itself. There was a drug-related break-in at our school and a number of my senior athletes were involved. It was another black mark on my program and I knew then that changes had to be made. How was I going to clean up the program? Though players from my team were involved, I saw this as not just a problem with the soccer team, but rather a problem in the community—one of those problems that schools, parents, and communities do not want to recognize. When I went to other coaches for help and suggestions they offered little support. Because my players were involved, it was my problem. I was on my own.

During that off-season, inspired by the NAIA Champions of Character program, I put together six core values for my program. I took some time to reflect and figure out what it was that I wanted the program to stand for. When people interacted with my players, watched them play, or had them in the classroom, what did I want them to notice? That next season we put up a sign at our practice site with these words on it:

- Respect
- Trust
- Quiet confidence
- Commitment
- Friendship
- FUN!

I sat down with my coaching staff at the time, which consisted of my great friends Roy Ramirez and Cory Clark, and discussed how we would implement and teach these values to our players. We changed the way we talked about team rules so that they were related to our values. We painted a picture of each value and made sure the players knew what each word meant and how it looked. Our boys' team made its first ever state soccer tournament that next season and the success over the next decade was unmatched in school history.

As we implemented this new character program with our soccer team, our district hired a new athletic director, Brian Skortz. A man of integrity, Skortz saw the value of this program and wanted to expand it across the entire athletic department. Through his leadership, we involved the school's entire roster of coaches and implemented the nine traits of our athletic program, expanding on the values we had shared with our soccer team. Having the implementation of the nine traits program come from the top was key to it becoming a cornerstone of our athletic department. The challenge for our athletic department was then to try and get each program on board. Not all of the school's coaches were ready for this doctrine, but we calmed some initial pushback by offering training and educational opportunities to help our coaches better understand what we were trying to accomplish. The message to our players was much more powerful when everyone received the same consistent expectations across all of their activities.

When I relocated and found a coaching position at Ida Baker High School in Cape Coral, Florida, I found that this school, like the one in Fond du Lac, did not have any department-wide athletic character program. I presented a plan to the school's athletic director, Brian Conn, who was very interested in the process. He gave me the green light to implement a character values program for my soccer program. My focus here was on six traits:

- Respect
- Responsibility
- Sportsmanship
- Integrity
- Service
- Team

© Greg Winkler

I learned very quickly that my inherited team at Ida Baker had a history of poor sportsmanship. Moving forward, I made sure that everything we did reflected our value systems. When a player reacted poorly to a referee call, we had a discussion about respecting the game. When we took an opponent lightly, we had a discussion about respecting our opponent. And when I heard rumors of substance abuse off the field, we had a discussion about respecting our bodies and our responsibility to the team.

My move to southwest Florida has allowed me the opportunity to work at a public charter high school, Florida SouthWestern Collegiate (FSWC). When I arrived, FSWC was under the guidance of a new principal, Matt Catanzarite, and his first order of business was to have our school establish a brand, which he labeled the Buc Brand for the school's Buccaneer mascot. The Buc Brand featured the following traits:

- Zest
- Curiosity
- Gratitude
- Self-control
- Social intelligence
- Optimism
- Grit

Florida SouthWestern Collegiate

We live and teach the brand at our school, and it was exciting for me to see this character value system taught and modeled throughout our school and not limited to just the athletic department.

Teams at the club and youth levels are worried about winning, while teaching character and sportsmanship have been put aside as many coaches believe it is not that important to team success. As I see it, character will win more games for you than any set piece or shooting drill will. Your program should be about more than just how many wins you can rack up. Establishing a true culture of character takes your program to an entirely new level. When your administrators and other staff members start to notice a change in your athletes, you can impact an entire school and community. Put character first and make it a cornerstone of your program.

4 ORGANIZATION AND PARENTS

A key element to successful coaching is organization, which encompasses a wide variety of areas. Some coaches are good at tactical organization, such as the formations they run, their set pieces, and their substitution plans. Other coaches are better at running practice sessions, planning parent meetings, and communicating well with players.

I have worked with, observed, and played for coaches who just went out and winged it in practice. Many young coaches who lack proper education come to practice with no plan in place and end up scrimmaging most of the practice. These coaches often miss key elements in their instruction, do not accomplish what they want to in practice, and finish too early because they did not have a good plan. Oftentimes their teams are not ready on game days and fail to reach their potential as the season wears on.

In Wisconsin, a local junior college offered soccer in our community and many of my players would attend the school for a year or two before transferring to another university. I was able to watch a few of these junior college games each season. The coach was very demonstrative on the sideline, yelling and screaming at both the officials and his own players for not making appropriate runs or for being in poor position on free kicks and corners, among other things. In conversations with my former players, they told me that they rarely listened to the coach because they did not have structured practices, and his rantings and ravings on the sidelines were for principles that were never dealt with in their training sessions.

It was obvious that the coach was knowledgeable about the game, but he was doomed by his organizational flaws and failure to put together good practice plans. He assumed his team knew what to do in game situations without ever coaching those situations.

It is imperative that a coach have a plan for everything involved in the operation of the team, which applies not only to practice sessions but also to parent and player meetings. In meeting with parents for the first time, it is important to be prepared and make a list of everything you want to cover. That meeting with the parents may be the only time you have them all together during the season, and it is important to be organized and present yourself in a positive manner. Forgetting a key element or talking point and then scrambling to find a way to disseminate that information at a later time can only bring headaches.

When I began my coaching career I did not have any kind of parental expectation presentation for my team. In one of my earlier seasons, my staff and I had a problem with the parents on the junior varsity teams and their sideline behavior. We scrambled to put a parental behavior plan in place but had difficulty getting the information out to every parent, which prolonged the problem.

One mistake many coaches make is to put parents in an adversarial role. How many times have you heard coaches say the job would be great if it weren't for the parents? Too often, I am sure, though this is not without some merit. Parents at youth sporting events have not always held up their end of the bargain in advancing coach–parent relations.

There are many types of parents that you'll come across on any given team. The most recognizable of these is the helicopter parent, one that has to control everything their child does. This protective parent hovers over the child's every action, always helping them with homework or even doing it for them. This parent makes all of the child's decisions for them, leading to a player who is not used to making decisions on his or her own and who needs constant instruction or reinforcement during the game.

A newer type of parent is the tiger parent, one that puts unreasonable pressures on their children so that nothing that they do will ever be good enough. This player will often be overcritical of their own performance and will go home to an even more brutal assessment of their game by that parent. This player tends to crack in stressful situations, especially if the parent is in the stands waiting to critique their every move.

I once had a very talented young girl come up through our club, and I couldn't wait for her to become part of my program. However, her father coached her select teams and our soccer club had many complaints about the way he treated the team, especially his own daughter.

As a result of the complaints, our club had to remove the father from our select program, which caused him to take his daughter to a different club and eventually a different high school. When this player was a junior at her new school, our teams met in the semifinal of an invitational tournament. We had an early 1-0 lead when our opponent was awarded a free kick from about 30 yards out. This young lady was very good and had quite a few goals at her new school, including a few on her deadly free kick. She lined up and took a beautiful shot to the near post that our keeper deflected before it could curve into the net.

Despite nearly scoring, the entire stadium heard her father yelling at her for missing the kick. She had four more free kicks during that game and didn't even come close on any of them. Her father had the traits of both a helicopter parent and a tiger parent, and it was clear that his screaming had affected her play. We won the game 4-0.

There are several other types of parents you'll no doubt encounter. The karaoke parent is one that tries to be their child's friend. This player will have a tendency not to follow rules because there are not any consequences at home when they disobey orders. The parent's desire for friendship means discipline becomes a foreign concept in the household.

Then there's the we parent, which is more prevalent today than ever before. This parent has done everything for their young player, including taken family vacations around their child's camps and tournaments. Everything the player has done is looked at as a shared accomplishment. I had a talented young forward who was scoring a lot of goals early into his junior year. In our eighth game of the year an ACL injury finished his season. This young man was determined to come back for his senior season and did so after working extremely hard throughout the next spring and summer.

He started off slow as it took him a few weeks to get back into the groove of competitive soccer, but he finished the season with a good number of goals and was hoping for some all-conference recognition. When the awards came out he was placed on the honorable mention team. Within minutes of the release I received text messages from his father and emails from his mother (neither parent knew the other was contacting me). Both parents asked the same question: "Why did we only get honorable mention?" They each had put in so much time and effort with their son's soccer career that they looked at the award as their own. Like most of these stereotypical parents, the we parent can be a either great asset or a royal pain in your butt.

I quit looking at parents as a problem and decided to be proactive and get them involved in the team. Parents want the best for their children; you just have to get them to realize that, as a coach, you are after the same thing. When I have parent meetings at the beginning of the season I have responsibilities or jobs I need help with. It may be running the concession schedule, planning team meals, being the team photographer or video person, or serving as a fundraising coordinator.

The key is to give the parent something else to focus on so that you can do the job you were hired to do. At my parent meeting, I tell them that there are four positions needed for us to play the game:

1. An official: our athletic director takes care of that.

2. A player: that is the responsibility of their child.

3. A coach: that is my job.

4. A fan: the only thing left, and that is for them.

I also stress the one voice philosophy. During competition the player is listening to one voice: mine. Parents can cheer and cheer loudly for their player and the other players on our team but only one voice is coaching and giving instructions, which is the head coach.

Organization and planning also help you stay on track when you are addressing your team, the parents, or the administration, especially when you find yourself in unfamiliar territory. When I have meetings with my boys' teams, I go through my list, we take care of business, and we adjourn. Our meetings are usually short and sweet and right to the point. After years of only coaching boys, the first time I had a girls' team meeting, it was a good thing I had that list prepared. What was supposed to be a 15-minute meeting ended up lasting over an hour. Because I underestimated the difference between coaching boys and girls, the meeting went off on so many tangents that without my list I surely would have forgotten something. I will expand on the differences between coaching boys and girls in a later chapter.

My recommendation to the coach who has a deficiency in the area of organization is to secure the help of an assistant who demonstrates strength in the area of team management. Your assistant can help you maintain the perception that you are organized, even if you are not.

I remember a banquet I put on early in my soccer coaching career that my wife attended. She has been very supportive and a big part of my program. I introduced all of my coaches and their spouses and told a little bit about each person. We had a great banquet and everyone left with a smile on his or her face, except for one very important person. You guessed it! I forgot to introduce my wife. My entire evening was just shattered. There was no way I was getting that night back. Since then, I always make sure to introduce my wife at the meetings. A little better organization on my part would have saved me numerous hours of make-up chores.

5 PRESEASON PACKET

My first soccer coaching experience at the high school level was as a freshman coach back in 1996. The varsity coach had a preseason packet that explained the team rules and expectations. After two seasons with the freshmen, I moved into the head varsity position and immediately adopted and amended the preseason document which would become the bible of my program.

On the cover of our team packet, I list the years that both our boys and girls teams have achieved conference, regional, and sectional championships. I also include the years our school has been recognized as a state sportsmanship award winner and the years we have received the NSCAA team academic award. Every time a player or parent references the information, the successes of the soccer program are right there in front of them. By putting our successes on the cover it reinforces that these are the expectations of the program. Academics and sportsmanship are just as important to the program as the championships we earn.

The cover also includes a listing of the coaching staff and their contact information, because it is important that our parents and players know how to communicate with us. The rest of the packet includes everything parents and players in our soccer program need to know. Most of the questions that parents may have are answered in the packet. Here are some things to consider when developing an information guide for your teams:

- **Starting dates of practice.** I include the dates when the girls' and boys' seasons begin, as well as the location and the apparel required for the tryout. As soon as the season is over, the start date for the next season is updated.
- **Physical exam information.** Our players need a current physical before they are allowed to participate, and we make sure that information is emphasized. Some schools offer free physicals, and we make sure they know that they can take advantage of that.
- **Mandatory meeting.** Prior to the start of each season, we hold a mandatory meeting for players and parents. This is the time to introduce staff and collect information. Many schools have mandatory paperwork prior to participation, and we disseminate that information at this meeting. It is also when I address parental expectations.
- **Team selection and tryout information.** This covers the number of teams we provide and the number of players we will keep. Information on tryout procedures and evaluations are also listed in this section.
- **Player responsibilities.** This section includes academic requirements and team conduct expectations.
- **Practice attendance expectations.** Attendance is very important for developing a successful team. Practice requirements and penalties for absences are detailed in this section.
- **Booster club requirements.** A program cannot survive without fundraising and this section describes what we will do to raise money as well as any player financial responsibility. Two of the

schools I coached at had a pay-for-play expectation, which we cover in that section as well.

- **Playing time philosophy.** This is a brief overview of what can be expected at the freshman, junior varsity, and varsity levels regarding playing time. Our lower level teams encourage development while the varsity level is highly competitive.

- **Award information.** Since we have individual awards at the end of the season, the packet includes varsity letter standards as well as all-conference and all-state possibilities. We give numerous other awards that are described in this area. Players who are involved in a drug- or alcohol-related incident during the season are not eligible for postseason awards.

- **Travel and bus behavior guidelines.** Expectations are put in the packet so everyone is clear about how the team is expected to act when we travel. One of the special travel rules we have is that everyone rides the bus to and from events. I want the players to communicate with each other and, win or lose, they share that experience on the way home. This also prevents their parents from coaching them all the way home after a contest.

- **Chain of command.** As the next chapter will explain, this is very important and parents, as well as players, need to hear it often.

- **Miscellaneous information.** This is where I list anything else which may be important, but did not fit in one of the categories. For example, I have a cell phone policy on bus trips. I purchase a small plastic tackle box at the beginning of the season and give it to the captains. They are allowed to decorate it however they want and this becomes the phone box. When we travel, I collect cell phones as the players arrive on the bus, and the box is stored until we head home. When we are within a half an hour of our return the phones are handed back so players can make sure their ride is on time. This fosters more camaraderie before and after games, and it gets them away from their electronics for a little while.

The packet is provided for all players and parents, and it reinforces the information that the coaches go over with their players. It is also very valuable to my athletic director, who has a copy of the document and can refer to it if there are any questions.

In addition to the team packet, my soccer program has now entered the technology age. We have a team Facebook page and a team Twitter account, and we have utilized some popular communication apps. Our school has a website where we keep the packet so there is an online version available.

A preseason packet is an excellent way to keep organized for the upcoming season. I make sure to review my packet every season to ensure that everything is current, appropriate, and up to date.

6 CHAIN OF COMMAND

One of the most important parts of my preseason packet is the chain of command, which is laid out in detail for the parents and players. After many years of dealing with parents, players, and administrators, it became imperative that a chain of command be established and followed by my staff and our school administration. It doesn't matter if you are a youth coach, middle school coach, high school or college coach—a chain of command is an essential tool to handle or avoid conflicts.

During my tenure at Fond du Lac High School we were fortunate enough to have a freshman, junior varsity, and a varsity soccer team. As the head coach, I had a varsity assistant as well as a junior varsity and freshman coach by my side. We had a superintendent, a building principal, four assistant principals, plus an athletic director that we had to answer to. Once the chain of command was established, it was very important for our administration to be on board with the plan and to understand how the chain of command worked. This understanding ensured the initiative's effectiveness.

Each season we explain the chain of command in detail at the parent meeting. While many people, including those in the administration, understand how a chain of command works, they do not always practice it.

Simply put, if players have an issue which they feel the need to discuss, it is their responsibility to talk with their coach. It is not the job of the parent to speak on their child's behalf; it is all on the player's shoulders. For example, if there is a conflict with a player on the freshman team, that player is expected to talk with his or her freshman coach. If the issue is not resolved, that player can request that the head coach of the program meet with them and the freshman coach. If the issue is still not resolved, then the parents may ask for a meeting with the freshman coach, the player, and the head coach of the program. The next step would then be the athletic director and eventually the building principal; however, this step should only be reached in extreme scenarios. To recap the steps:

1. Player meets with team coach

2. Player meets with team coach and program's head coach

3. Player meets with coach(es) and parent

4. Player meets with parent, coach(es), and athletic director

5. Player meets with parent, coach(es), athletic director, and principal

When this process is put in place and followed, most of the issues are resolved when the player has a conversation with the coach (step 1). There are far too many parents who feel they have to fight their children's battles at a time when young men and women need to learn these communication skills for themselves.

The only way this chain works is if the coach, athletic director and the administration understand the process and allow it to work. There are many administrators who hear a complaint from a parent and feel the need to fix the matter right away to appease the parent. For the chain to work as intended, the administrators need to find out if the complaining parent had their student-athlete speak to the coach first. If not, the parent should be instructed to follow the chain of command. The administrator can emphasize to the parent that if doing so does not resolve the issue, it will eventually come back to the administration. By following the chain, the parents learn that this is the way to empower their children in their activities.

I learned that I needed to implement and educate our administration about a chain of command early in my high school coaching career. Our conference did not allow us to keep juniors on the junior varsity team and I had a large number of seniors on the varsity team that year. With our roster size limitations, I was not allowed to keep some of those junior players who would still have a chance to play as seniors the following year. While the players who made the team participated in a scrimmage, I met with each junior player who would not make the varsity. Each player was spoken to individually and given an explanation of why he was not making the varsity team that season. I let the players know that I hoped they would continue to play and I would welcome them to come out again the next season.

One of those young men had a very poor attitude, which played into the decision of letting him go. I explained the situation to him and let him know that if he worked on his attitude in the off-season, he could try out again and contribute as a senior. Our conversation was not what he expected to hear. After much verbal abuse by the player, both in my face and across the practice field as he left, the situation escalated.

By the time the player got home, his story was not the same as what had actually happened during the session. I did not have any other staff available that evening and only other players to support what had actually occurred. Instead of making an appointment to see me after he calmed down, the player's mother went directly to the principal. The principal was a close personal friend of this parent and without a chain of command in place, the principal felt she had to listen to the parent instead of directing the parent to the process of the chain of command.

It was a very difficult two weeks for me as a young coach. A meeting was called and the issue made it all the way to the superintendent's office. Fortunately, the issue was resolved during this meeting and the player remained off the team. Immediately following the incident, I sat down with my athletic director and instituted my chain of command.

When putting a chain of command in place it is important to remind the athletic director and administrators how you want complaints handled. Many sound athletic programs have a good chain of command in place directed and enforced by the school's athletic director, but it is still a good idea to remind your superiors that you are making the chain of command a priority.

A recent example happened when I left Wisconsin and took the girls' soccer coach position at George Jenkins High School in Lakeland, Florida. After my initial parent meeting where I provided my expectations and laid out my chain of command, there was a parent that had some questions during the first weeks of practice. Our school had an athletic director as well as an activities director, both of whom oversaw different aspects of the school's events. The activities director had previously held the athletic director position and had built some relationships with parents in that community.

The parent was questioning some of the things that were implemented within the program and voiced her concerns with the activities director.

I was immediately called into the director's office the next day. After defending myself and answering the complaints, I reminded the activities director of my chain of command. I asked the director to support the process as we moved forward. After the meeting I sent a strong message to the parents of my team about the chain of command. The process was new to them and some remedial education was needed.

Parents often have to be reminded of the chain of command as well. One of my recent girls' teams had your typical helicopter parent. This father had been talking to me about his daughter's talents since she was in elementary school. As this young lady got closer and closer to high school, he would find ways to bump into me and share her latest soccer successes. When he told me how the local parochial high school had guaranteed his budding national team player a starting spot as a freshman should she go there, I continued to listen. It was never my policy to promise anything.

She chose our school and tried out at as a freshman, and her father was at every training session during the tryout. When teams were made the father was right there to see his dejected daughter bypass the freshman squad only to be placed on the secondary JV team. We divided the girls into their respective teams and gave them a quick break before they went for a short practice with their new team.

During these practices, the father asked to speak with me. I told him he would have to wait until the training session was over. While the freshman and JV teams finished their training, I kept the varsity practice going a little longer just to keep him waiting. When he approached and started to ask about the team placement, I told him he had to stop for a moment. His daughter had been placed on the JV team. If she had some questions, according to the chain of command, she needed to go speak with the JV coach first.

He wasn't very happy with me, but he had heard the chain of command speech multiple times—which my athletic director and administration supported—so he had no choice. His daughter went on to have a nice high school career and he eventually learned to let her make her own soccer decisions and start enjoying the game more.

Because of instances like these, I believe establishing a chain of command should be a high-priority item if you want to last in the coaching business. With a good chain of command in place, you and your staff are allowed to do what you do best: COACH!

7 SETTING TEAM GOALS

If there is one area covered in this book that every coach is probably already familiar with, it is setting your team goals. It is imperative that a goal-setting meeting take place once you have picked your squad for the season. What expectations for outcomes and results do your players have for the season? Are your expectations the same as your players? How do you combine your goals with those of the team? These are some questions you should explore with your team during a goal-setting meeting. Coaching a team without goals for the season would be like taking a trip across the country without a road map or a destination.

Deciding how to handle this meeting is very important. It does not do any good if your goals as a coach do not mesh with those of your players. When I took over the boys' program at Ida Baker High School, many of my players were content to have a varsity uniform. My goals of competing for a district championship and having a winning season were not on the radar of a player content just to make the roster.

In my goal-setting meetings in the past, I was the facilitator, helping to guide the team to goals that I believed were attainable. I believed that I had a pretty good feel for where my team was and what they could accomplish and believed it was my responsibility to challenge the team to set higher, but still attainable, goals and then transfer that challenge from our meeting to the practice field.

However, I have found a more inclusive way to set goals, giving more of the ownership of those goals to the players. I pick a date after the team selection but prior to our first contest and, about halfway through that day's practice, I bring the team in for a break. The team splits up into five or six groups with a senior leading each group. I provide poster board with our school logo centered in the middle and allow the groups five to ten minutes to come up with a few goals.

Their instructions are to brainstorm anything they hope to accomplish throughout that season. Whatever they think of as a goal is then written inside the logo. It can be a win-loss number, a district or conference championship, or the chance to break a school record or to achieve the academic award. Nothing is off the table. Outside of the logo, the groups are to list any possible distractions that could come between the team and the goals we will set. Listing the distractions is a very valuable discussion tool for the team.

One season, my girls' team was in the sectional final, one game away from a berth in the state tournament. We were well-prepared and the team was, as far as I was concerned, ready to play and earn us that state tourney opportunity. Within the first ten minutes of the game, my senior forward had three great goal-scoring opportunities, but she failed to convert all three attempts. On the other end of the field, my senior goalkeeper was not her usual brick-wall self and allowed three goals in the first half. Instead of having a comfortable lead we found ourselves down 3-0. I made some substitutions with underclassman and we made a run at the victory, but we could not erase that early deficit. We lost the game.

On the bus ride home, I overheard some conversations and realized that if we had won the contest, we would have played our first game of the state tournament at seven o'clock the following Thursday, a time and date that coincided with our seniors' high school graduation. We had eleven seniors on the squad that year; I believe that distraction and our inability to address the concerns cost our team a chance to play in the state tournament.

For reasons such as this, we list the distractions on the goal sheets. When the team is done with our group work, I bring everyone back together, and each group presents their goals and distractions. We discuss the listings and narrow down the goals that are most important to us all as a team. The goals are then copied on a new sheet, laminated, and kept in each player's equipment bag as a constant reminder about what we want to accomplish.

We also identify all of the distractions that players listed and we discuss those distractions and how to prevent them from getting in our way. If the graduation ceremony is an issue down the road, we discuss it as a possible problem. Often we discuss substance abuse, school breaks, social activities, and other school-related commitments.

Once we have decided on our goals, they become our road map—a guide that will help our team reach its destination. The coaching staff and the players can now surround themselves with people who will help them achieve their goals and avoid possible pitfalls along the way. Allowing your players to be part of the goal-setting process also provides empowerment and a chance for the players to be part of the process.

8 SELECTING THE TEAM

One of the most exciting times of the season for me is that first day of tryouts or practice: a new beginning. Every year is exciting to see which players will show up for tryouts, which players' off-season work improved their game, and which players are going to surprise the staff with their improvements. On the flip side, the tryout phase of the season is the most stressful time of the year with tough decisions to be made, such as assigning players to the different squads and deciding how many to keep on the roster. Roster cuts can be just as stressful to the coaching staff as they are for the players.

In my early varsity coaching seasons, our athletic department only allowed a varsity roster of eighteen. In addition to being a fairly standard number for a soccer squad, from a practical standpoint, we were only budgeted for eighteen uniforms. We were able to keep larger numbers at the freshman and junior varsity levels, however we could still only dress eighteen players. Fortunately for our program's development, our state association expanded the state tournament rosters to 22 players and our athletic department added enough uniforms to keep more kids involved.

If numbers and talent allow, I now keep the maximum of 22 players on my varsity squads. When I was in Wisconsin, we were fortunate to be able to provide opportunities at three levels, whereas in Florida we only have two. I have always tried to find spots for as many players as possible. Seldom did we cut freshman, sophomores, or juniors; often the only players we cut were seniors who did not do what was needed to help the team.

It has always been my position to put the best 22 players on the varsity squad. When I started coaching, our school board dictated that you had to keep upperclassman at the varsity level unless an underclassman was clearly better. I stay pretty true to that guideline even today. On the boys' side, in a well-established program it should be extremely difficult for a freshman to make the varsity team. If my program is working properly and we are developing athletes, the upperclassman should be bigger, stronger, and more talented, and have better game intelligence. A sophomore usually only makes the team if I believe they will earn at least half a game of playing time. If that is not the case, that player is better off at a lower level where they will play almost every minute while also getting the opportunity to gain leadership experience. On the girls' side it is different. I have had many female players that earned varsity spots as freshman and dominated throughout their high school career. I will expand on that in a later chapter.

Through years of trial and error, I have learned that if senior players will not play significant time, they ultimately become unhappy and can become a distraction to the team. Oftentimes, seniors who are in jeopardy of not making the varsity have been involved in the program at the lower levels for years. Relationships have been formed and it is tough to tell them that there is no place for them on the roster as a senior. If I have a player that has been involved in the program and really wants to be part of the team but does not have the skills to help us on the field, we have a chat. I sit down with the player and explain where they stand in relationship to the rest of the players trying out. We talk about their performance and their expectations, and I ask them specifically what they can do to help should we keep them. During this meeting I make it very clear that while they cannot expect playing time, their humor, leadership, and dedication to the team can add something to our squad that may not be reflected in playing time. If after our talk I think it will be difficult to make the season significant for them, they will not be part of the team. It sounds cold but there is nothing more damaging to a team than a disgruntled player thinking only of themselves.

At Ida Baker High School in Florida, I was hired the day before the season began and I did not know the players very well. One of the seniors trying out was a little out of shape but had a great attitude. Fortunately I had a few other senior leaders that helped provide some insight on different players as I whittled down my final squad. One of the seniors approached me and asked for my thoughts regarding the out-of-shape player. It was quite obvious that he would not make the team as we approached the end of the tryout period. The senior that approached me asked that I consider keeping that player, arguing that he was a great kid and that his attitude would be great for the team.

That led to a chat with that player, where I asked what he could bring to the table and how could he help our team. We had a great conversation and he became a member of the squad; he was a great teammate and even earned some playing time. His value to our team was not so much on-the-field performance as it was what he brought to our practices, our bus rides, and our team functions. The season was significant for him and the bond we created and the memories we shared will be part of us for the rest of our lives.

On the flip side, there have been seniors that I have kept on the squad because I wanted to reward their loyalty to the program even if their skill level was not what was needed to compete at the level we were at. When I have the chat with them, the player is often excited and accepting of the role laid out before them and are grateful to be part of the squad. However, as the season progresses, some of these players become more and more disgruntled, and their complaining, questioning, or poor attitude begins to seep into the squad. Many times it is not the player's fault. The player knows and accepts the role, but his or her parent has trouble watching the game from the stands and starts to question the coach's decisions and actions. It has become part of my program policy that if a senior is not going to play a significant amount of time and there is any question whatsoever regarding their attitude, I will cut them after the tryout period. I would prefer to take the heat early in the year rather than have a player or their parent affect the chemistry of the team later on in the season.

During one of my boys' seasons, I kept a senior who had been with the program all the way through. He was an average player but had a great attitude, and unfortunately for him there was a very talented class of players in the grade behind him. His playing opportunities would be limited in close games, however we were good enough that season for him to get some quality playing time. His biggest strength was his accuracy on penalty kicks and he was a lock for a top-five spot anytime we encountered a penalty shoot-out. We made a deep run in the playoffs that season with two shoot-outs along the way. This senior made both chances and helped us advance in both contests. He was thrilled to be part of those victories, despite the fact that he saw very little playing time during the actual games. Despite the player's positive attitude, I received a not-so-friendly note from his mother after the season was completed, because she was not privy to the conversation that I had with her son prior to the start of the season and he chose not to share the conversation with her. In this instance, at least to this mom, the player was more important than the team. Her son had a role on the team and he did an outstanding job in that role. As a parent, it was her job to recognize that and allow him to enjoy the experience. If the player had a concern, a discussion – following the Chain of Command would've have taken place. Therefore, the player's season of significance may have been negitively affected by his mother's dissappointment.

Once the team is selected, the players begin competing for a spot on the first eleven. As previously mentioned, if numbers and talent allow, I keep 22 players on the varsity squad. While it is often hard to keep a squad of 22 players happy in regards to playing time, I like the competitive environment that we can create within the varsity 22. Once roles are established I can refer to the group as the first eleven and second eleven. Players move back and forth between the groupings based on practice and game performance, injuries, possible opponent match-ups, and other circumstances that may pop up. My second eleven is very supportive of the first because of our strong team-building structure, which reinforces the fact that we are all part of the same team, striving for the same goals.

To help balance playing time and provide second eleven players with in-game experience, I have a three-goal/twenty-minute rule. If our squad is up by three goals or down by three goals with twenty minutes to play, I will substitute the entire squad. Throughout the match I make substitutions to keep players fresh and provide opportunities for everyone, but in a tight match that may only affect the next three or four players. With the three-goal/twenty-minute rule, players know that when the team gets the desired outcome or we fall badly behind, they will get their chance to play.

Most coaches have heard the slogan, "We are not rebuilding, we are reloading." The second eleven is primarily made up of underclassmen and, in essence, we are training them to step in and be the first eleven in the following season. We have seen average junior players who worked hard on the second eleven develop into outstanding senior players the next year. The 22-player roster is also very effective for practices, especially if you do a lot of in-game training and coaching. It also provides some very competitive 11-v-11 training sessions to finish practice.

While the tryout and team selection process is by far the most stressful and emotional time of the year for most coaches, it allows a coach to have some great conversations with individuals if they use that time effectively. Laying out your expectations and keeping things consistent from year to year creates a culture that will help make the process less stressful and the season more enjoyable.

9 DEALING WITH THE PRIMA DONNA ATHLETE

I have played, coached, and observed countless athletic contests over the course of my lifetime. Many of the games I have coached in and observed have been at the youth and high school level. I have witnessed players behaving with poor sportsmanship, bad attitudes, or what I would call the "me" mentality. With that behavioral performance comes the reaction of the coach and how the coach handles the player behavior.

The manner in which a youth coach handles such behavior from an athlete will have an impact on that player's future teams. If the coach does not deal with the behavior effectively, coaches at the high school level will have a much more difficult time with that player as a teenager. This is the dreaded prima donna athlete.

Many times this young athlete is physically more mature than his or her classmates and is able to run faster, jump higher, throw harder, you name it. Due to the player's superior talent, his or her peers are drawn to their personality and will defer to that athlete. The prima donna's peers allow him or her to get away with more than others, even if they know the behavior demonstrated by that athlete is inappropriate. The prima donna's peers hold the gifted player to a different standard than themselves.

In most cases, the gifted athlete moves onto competitive youth programs where they continue to excel. Many of the coaches at these youth levels are parents, young adults, or students looking to gain experience in the coaching ranks, and are often more concerned with game results than they are with the physical and emotional development of their players.

If you sit down to watch a youth basketball game in which you do not know any of the kids playing, it will not take long for you to pick out the better players. You'll see that the better players get away with making mistakes for which an inferior player might be removed from the court. As the player gets older and realizes that their talent level allows them to get away with certain things, they may start to get verbal, talking back to the coach or the officials because there are no repercussions. Many times coaches allow negative behavior because without that player in the lineup the chance for a victory is diminished.

At the high school level, if this player has gone unchecked, they become a real problem in the program. Their behaviors are now a part of them that their peers accept because of the talent they possess. Parents likewise have watched this player grow up and have also tolerated the behavior because of the success that comes along with the player's talents.

When I deal with the behavior at the varsity level, I then face resistance not only from the player but from his teammates and their parents as well. So how do you deal with the prima donna player? First, you must identify the behavior and bring it to the athlete's attention. Take the time to teach the athlete how to behave or control themselves to prevent the behavior. Make sure the athlete understands there will be consequences if the behavior continues.

One of my former players—an extremely competitive, very self-motivated, perfectionist-type—was a 4.0 student in high school and went on to play four years of college soccer. He had difficulty, however, in dealing with referees and anything that he considered to be a bad call. He would often throw his arms in the air and question the referee's calls. In the first three games of his sophomore season he had already picked up three yellow cards. I pulled him aside and told him that anytime I saw that behavior, he would be substituted and brought off the field.

He had demonstrated these behaviors since he was ten years old, but he had been allowed to carry on that way for every coach he played for because he was a talented player. It was going to be difficult for him to suddenly make an adjustment in the way that he approached the game. Over the next four games, every time I saw that behavior begin to take shape, I would remove him from the field. He would sit for a period of time and go back in. He was a fierce competitor and did not like to come off the field, so he had to make a decision: If he wanted to play soccer, he had to get his emotions under control.

During the fifth game after our discussion, his argumentative behavior was starting to surface again. A substitute went to the line so he could cool off. He realized what was happening and knew he was coming off, causing him to go berserk on the field. He was given a red card in the contest and his teammates had to play short the remainder of the game. I did not talk to him right away; his team was very disappointed in him, compounded by his own disappointment in himself. This occurred during a tournament, so between games we talked and he saw how the red card was really given for displaced anger. The referee thought the player was yelling him, but in reality he was very upset with me because I kept subbing him out of games. After our discussion about his self-control I made a new agreement with him. I told him I would loosen the reins I had on him as long as he did a better job of focusing on what he could control and not on the officials. He did not pick up another card that season—or the next two that he played for me—and he became an all-state player his senior year.

Every coach can recognize poor behavior, yet many do not think it warrants removing the player from the game if that player is essential to the outcome. In failing to address the behavior, they allow bad habits to form that could prove far more detrimental to the team in the long run.

During a regional championship game, my team played against an opponent that had a very talented midfielder with a reputation for his poor attitude. He was constantly chirping and questioning the official's calls. I had spoken to the coach of that team a few weeks prior to our contest and he talked about this player and the problems he had in dealing with his behavior all season. The coach did not have a behavior plan and was not prepared, or willing, to try and get his midfielder's actions under control.

In our game, his star player got on the referee immediately, picking up a yellow card early in the first half. The player was sent off and his coach rewarded the behavior by returning him to the field almost immediately. There were many more times in the first half that the player could've been sent off, however the official did not want to send this player to the bench again knowing it would be a double yellow and the end of his game, and possibly season. We were down 1-0 with five minutes to play in the match when a foul was committed by our opponent 30 yards from the goal. This prima donna player argued the call and then kicked the ball away, the last straw for the referee who had been hearing from him all game. The referee issued the second yellow and off the field this young man went. We scored on the free kick and eventually advanced to the sectional round on penalty kicks. The talented midfielder would have surely been one of the team's five penalty kickers, but did not get the chance. It was a perfect example of a player being allowed to get away with poor behavior all season and eventually damaging his team's chances of extending the season.

What further damage was done to that program? How many young players observed this young man's behavior all through the season without penalty? How many more seasons will the coach have to endure this behavior because he let it persist? Establishing core values for your program helps to hold your players accountable. It can be uncomfortable to confront an athlete about his or her behavior, but by establishing core values at the onset of the season, you can open the lines of communication with a potential prima donna and end the poor behavior before it ultimately contributes to the end of your season.

10 MAKING THE CUT

As mentioned, along with the excitement of the beginning of the season comes the stressful player evaluations and team assignments, which include cutting players from the team. What is the best way to tell a player that they will not be part of the program for the new season? Everyone has a plan for this part of the job, and some are better than others. After many years of trial and error and observations from other coaches, I found a system that has worked for me. If you are coaching for significance then you are always thinking with a kids-first mindset.

Tryout periods vary from school to school. In Wisconsin the high school season is short, with our first contest coming only eight days after the start of the season. Florida, on the other hand, provides a two-week training window prior to any contests so I have a little more time and therefore take five days for evaluations. Additionally, we get a chance to see players during summer league games, captain's practices, and summer camps. Our staff usually has a pretty good idea of what each player is bringing to the team when they come to practice, but there are always surprises that keep the tryout process interesting.

Once we finish the player evaluations, we get ready to select the teams and finish with 11-v-11 games. The players are mixed randomly and matched up against other players while we make final decisions. We set it up so the final 11-v-11 game is made up of the 22 players who will be placed on the varsity squad. During this 11-v-11 process, my assistant and I speak to each player as they are resting off the field. I personally speak with each player about the tryout process, how they performed, and what their strengths and weaknesses are, and finally let them know which team they are on. Players are given a chance to ask questions and give feedback to coaches, and some get quite emotional when they find out there is not a spot for them or they are placed at a level below their expectation. We make sure each player has a chance to express themselves and that they leave knowing that these decisions are not personal (girls often think we do not like them if they don't make the team).

I have learned through this process what it means to double up. We make certain to employ the double-up tactic whenever we, the coaches, speak to a player about sensitive issues like playing time, player performance, or behaviors on or off the field. This means that there are always two coaches present in these communications. This technique helps to protect the coach in he said-she said situations and give support should a player overreact to some less than favorable news. If doubling up is not part of your communication plan, it is something you should add immediately.

These player/coach meetings accomplish a number of things and can often clear up any hard feelings between the player and coach. At the high school level, players may also be students in the coach's class, which makes it even more imperative to meet as player and coach to avoid any lingering hostility between student and teacher. The players generally appreciate the honest and fair assessment about their tryout performance. When coaches make personal contact with them it also helps maintain a positive relationship with that player in the future. It is very important to me that a player who is eliminated from our program continues to support soccer and cheer for his or her friends on the team. It is the coach's responsibility to communicate with them and help them deal with this personal setback.

As an example, during one of these player/coach meetings, a young man, Vernon Farley, really wanted to be part of our program. He had worked very hard preparing for the tryout and had been in the program as a junior varsity player the previous two seasons. Vern was well-liked by his peers and was a great teammate. Unfortunately he was not as fit as he needed to be and he was a late bloomer athletically. As our conversation took place it was quite obvious that Vern would do anything to help our team and not only did he want to be part of the team, on some level he *needed* to be part of it.

I gave Vern the opportunity to be our manager. Though we were only provided 22 uniforms by the athletic department, our fundraising efforts allowed me to purchase a uniform for him. Vern was a great manager and because of our team's success, we were able to get Vern in quite a few contests. Vern and I still communicate to this day and he certainly had a season of significance.

Far too often, coaches avoid face-to-face meetings with players when things are difficult because they can be uncomfortable. Many coaches I know post final cuts on a website or post a sign on the locker room door. While a website posting may allow a player to take the news privately, it gives no feedback or closure to the process if the player was cut. Posting on a bulletin board for all to see is even more stressful for the player that is cut, especially if they are surrounded by peers when viewing. This is not only uncomfortable for the player that was cut, but it is also uncomfortable for their friends that made the team. Once again, like the website posting, there is no closure for the player and a good relationship with that coach is damaged forever.

When my youngest son Brent was in seventh grade he was encouraged to try out for the middle school basketball team. The school had a team of ten that traveled throughout the region and played other middle schools. Beyond the middle school team, a recreational league was offered that gave opportunities to those who either did not make the school team or just wanted to have fun playing basketball in a looser environment.

It was a fairly large middle school and the seventh-grade coach had two cut periods. On both occasions, the coach posted names on a sheet and hung it on the bulletin board in the gym before the boys left for the night. Brent was a good athlete and made the first cut, and while he was happy he was on the list, he felt bad for his friends that were not. After a few more days the second round of cuts were made the same way. This time his name was not on the list. A devastated seventh grader came home with no explanation as to why he was dropped over others. In his mind players were kept who played with lesser skill and game intelligence.

The coach, a very popular teacher, told the boys that if they had any questions about the process he would be available in the morning to discuss them. Here was his mistake: being a middle school teacher and dealing with children at that stage of development, he should have been aware that seventh-grade boys are not going to volunteer to have a conversation about their shortcomings. Instead, they would be upset, complain to their friends, and choose another activity. I sent a message to the coach asking that he have a conversation with my son about the decision. My son was going to continue to play recreational basketball, and try and make the team in eighth grade, but his enthusiasm was dampened and I wanted the coach to have the conversation with him. The coach agreed and told my son his weaknesses, what he could do to improve upon them, and how he thought playing on the recreational team would allow him more playing time and a chance to develop his leadership skills.

Those were great comments and comments that should have been shared immediately. If the coach had not had the conversation, my son probably would have ended up quitting basketball altogether and putting that extra time into video games. The worst part was that a great student–teacher relationship had been severely damaged by delaying the conversation.

Young coaches often glean from their own past coaches and what they observed as players themselves. If a young coach was a good player himself, he or she would have never experienced a moment like my son Brent did and would not know how to handle that situation as a coach. This coach changed the way he selected teams after seeing how effective a conversation could be and he continues to be a positive influence on the middle school kids he works with.

It is unrealistic for a coach at any level to expect a player to come and seek them out. Players work hard to make our teams and they deserve feedback on their efforts during tryouts and throughout their seasons. As a coach and evaluator, you are the expert, and your players deserve to know that you respect them enough to communicate with them.

It may be uncomfortable talking to your players about not making the team. Explaining a shortcoming to a young athlete is not always an easy task, but if you take the time to have that conversation you could avoid some angry parental calls and meetings with your athletic director in the future. Just do yourself a favor and make sure you not only have the conversation, but that you double up when doing so.

Anson Dorrance, the University of North Carolina soccer coach, uses a system of daily ratings of his players to drive competition. Every challenge, every drill, and every effort are scored, evaluated, ranked, and posted for every player to see. It works very well for Coach Dorrance as he is able to recruit the top talent in the country and he can bring in that highly competitive personality to his team. A coaching colleague of mine adopted this practice for his high school girls' team. After each session during the tryout phase he posted times and skill results, assigned them scores, and had a daily ranking of each player. Every girl knew where they were in the tryout process, and the players were under the assumption a line would be drawn at eighteen and that would be the squad.

One of the players was in the top five after day one and remained in the top ten after the second day with one day of tryouts remaining. The final day was pretty subjective and based on 4-v-4 play. The coach was not confident in this player's ability as a varsity player and she went from being a top-ten player to number 25, keeping her off the varsity squad. The player, after seeing the updated chart, was very upset. She went home and was back almost immediately with an irate father. The coach had put himself in a dangerous situation. By the time the father came back everyone else had left and the coach was alone with an angry father. He now had to justify why this girl— who was in the top ten the day before—did not make the varsity team. The player had memorized every other players' times and scores, and put this coach in a very uncomfortable position. The player, only a sophomore, chose not to play junior varsity and left the program for good.

Even though the coach was trying to push the competitive envelope and be transparent with his team selections, he had not thought through the process enough to handle the situation he put himself in. He also did not keep an assistant around until he left so he could double up at all times. There are some important lessons to be learned from this situation:

- In high school, we are not dealing with heavily recruited college athletes.
- There is a time and place for posting results for players to look at. When you want to include some subjectivity, it may be best to keep the results to yourself.
- Always have an assistant coach around when there is a potential for player issues.

The bottom line for me is similar to the Golden Rule: Always treat players with respect, just as you would want your own son or daughter to be treated by another coach. Making cuts is stressful enough as it is — don't make the process any harder than it needs to be.

11 THE DIFFERENCE BETWEEN BOYS AND GIRLS

There are fundamental differences between coaching boys and girls that could fill the pages of an entire coaching book. By no means am I proclaiming to be an expert in this area, but I have discovered some interesting traits in relating to both genders from a coaching perspective.

I have coached both boys and girls in the highly competitive high school varsity environment, beginning as a varsity boys' coach for eight years before the girls' varsity position opened up as well. In Wisconsin, the boys' season takes place in the fall while the girls' season is in the spring, allowing me to coach both genders at the high school level. When the announcement was made that the girls program would soon be my responsibility, many of my peers warned me that I needed to be ready. "Girls are so different than boys," they said. "Be ready for a culture shock."

As a father of four boys and no girls, I took their cautions into consideration and picked up a few books on gender differences to try and prepare myself. What was the big deal? How could girls be that much different to coach? Will my interactions really be different with my boys' team than they are with my girls' team? The research I did was helpful, but there was nothing like on-the-job training.

As mentioned in an earlier chapter, I noticed a difference as early as my initial team meeting. With the boys' team, I would set aside fifteen minutes for the meeting and it would be over in ten. The boys did not want to sit around and talk. "Cover what you need to, Coach, and let's get out of here."

My first meeting with my new girls' team was an entirely different experience. Team selections had just been made so I scheduled the school conference room so I could get the girls together and map out a plan for the season. The previous coach did things differently than what I had planned, and I wanted to spend a little time to get us moving in this new direction. The room was scheduled for 30 minutes and it was a good thing it wasn't booked after that. That first 30-minute meeting took over an hour. I learned that whatever time I had initially planned for my team meetings, I had better double it.

Girls spend more time planning pregame meals, figuring out what to wear on game days, and organizing potential team outings. When we traveled to an overnight tournament, the girls wanted all the details right away: room assignments, where we were eating, what we were doing in our free time, and so on. The girls were concerned with senior night and who would decorate the bus on away trips. The boys never decorated the bus, and I took care of senior night.

Then there's the team photo day. At the start of every season with the boys, I would get a date and time from the athletic director when our team picture would be taken. The boys would start practice, change quick, take the picture, and finish practice. We were able to get something accomplished during our practice session. The girls, on the other hand, made the team photo the top priority. We could not practice beforehand because it would mess up their hair and by the time we finished the team shot and individual pictures, our allotted practice time was over. Now, when coaching girls, picture day is a non-training day for us.

Team building and team bonding activities are very important to me. Planning and organizing these activities for a boys' team is time consuming. If I didn't take the time to plan them, we would not have them. While my boys' teams really enjoy and appreciate the activities, they would not take the time to organize anything on their own. My girls' teams have always been just as excited and appreciative of those efforts as well, however if I did not have something planned, they would often organize things on their own. It is better if the coach is involved because girls will sometimes plan functions that do not include the entire team and could cause some hard feelings. Planning these extra team functions is also a way of showing your teams that you care about them off the field as well as on it.

While in Wisconsin, my boys' team would often play in tournaments that required an overnight stay at a hotel. These were great trips and we often went to a nice restaurant or visited a local attraction to make the trip special. These functions were always fun and provided great team moments. The girls' team at the school enjoyed hearing about our trips and wanted to have the same experiences, but the coach at the time did not want to take on the responsibility of an overnight trip with high school players. When I took over the girls' team at the same school, the first thing the girls did was approach me about overnight tournaments.

That led to a great event with a colleague of mine, John Ziperski of Sugar River girls' soccer. Coach Ziperski is always looking to make the game bigger than going out on the field and playing, so we took turns hosting a quad tournament, bringing in two additional teams for a weekend event. We would have a game Friday evening, and after the game the host school would put on a spaghetti dinner for every team at the tournament. These events bring opposing teams together and make the event more meaningful, not just about who wins the next afternoon. Girls are more receptive to multiple team get-togethers than boys are.

Training is another example of gender differences. When you give instructions to a group of boys and then go from group to group to oversee the work, they follow the coach's instructions for a brief period and then start to do their own thing. Boys have to be constantly corrected and reminded to stay on task during practice and are more apt to think they know it all already and just start playing. Boys will also be more prone to get away with as much as possible on fitness tests and drills. Girls, on the other hand, have a desire to perfect whatever drill or concept the coach puts before them. I often have female athletes apologize to me if they think they are letting me down in a training session. It is very seldom a male athlete apologizes for not hitting a fitness target.

Ultimately, the differences between boys and girls are surface issues. If you treat people with respect and show them that you care about them as individuals, there really is no difference. It comes down to respecting them and building relationships with them. I am a transformational coach and believe in the development of the individual and the team as a whole. Screaming at individual players, disrespecting young athletes, and putting them down has never been in my wheelhouse. Many coaches have success through intimidation and fear, and while that can sometimes work with young men, it seldom works with young women.

I heard a story from a college volleyball coach once about taking on a successful women's program. He was a former boys' coach and had accepted a position with a top-level team. They were very successful and found themselves in the conference championship where a win meant a trophy and a spot in the national tournament. He pushed his team hard but never really had to light a fire under them because of their strong play. In the finals, the match was tied at two games apiece and his team was down in the fifth and final set; his star player had been off all weekend and he decided to call a timeout and address his team. During the timeout, he did what he had done with many boys' teams in the past and ripped apart his star player, thinking she would "man up," respond to his criticism, take on the challenge, and bring home the title. Instead, the opposite happened. His team of young women looked at him in disbelief, shocked that the coach was attacking one of them individually. The team shut down mentally and gave up the next ten points, finishing as the runner-up. The coach had made a drastic mistake in dealing with girls. Instead of rallying as a team, they rallied with each other and turned against the coach. He learned a very tough lesson that afternoon.

Girls are focused on the process and relationships. You can build great girls' teams if you put together a plan that involves growing together not only as players but also as teammates. When girls feel accepted by their teammates and their coaches, their performance increases. Boys are more result-oriented and outcome-focused. Boys earn their acceptance from their peers based on performance. Challenge a young man and he will do his best to fulfill that challenge. His teammates will expect it from him as well and feed off of that desire.

One season I had a girls' team that, on paper, could challenge for a conference championship. We decided that we would put together our toughest schedule in school history and really prepare ourselves for a deep playoff run. After our first five non-conference games against ranked opponents we were 0-5, each loss by one goal. We played six more games, two of them against our strongest conference foes, and won one, tied two, and lost three more by a single goal. Our record was 1-8-2 and I needed to do something. Our players had lost confidence, our star player was underperforming, and we looked destined to end the season early. Being aware of the plight of the volleyball coach I had spoken with, I was careful not to call out any individual players. I was positive with the team in practice and we worked on correcting our issues.

On a Wednesday near the end of the season, after a loss the previous day and another tough game the following night, we had a school-wide senior athletic banquet scheduled for the evening. We had practice before the banquet and it was going nowhere; our eight seniors were worried about what to wear to the banquet and the entire team felt distracted. I had seen enough and abruptly ended the practice. I told the girls to meet me at the bench area near our storage shed before I sent them home. As I walked to the shed, I rehearsed my speech to the team.

It was time to come down hard on them. I chewed out that group of 22 young ladies like never before. I slapped the wall of the building, frothed at the mouth, and gave my best fire-and-brimstone speech. I let them go and I walked away. I had no idea how they were going to react to my tongue-lashing. As I arrived at the event that evening, none of my players would look at me. I thought they were mad at me, when in fact they all felt as though they had disappointed me.

After the initial shock, they realized that my rant was not personal. Not one girl was called out as an individual, but rather I addressed overall team behaviors and attitudes. It was very important that there was passion in my speech, but that I kept emotion out of it. We had lost our way as a team, but I did not like them any less as individuals. Because of the strong relationships that we had built during the season we were able to get back on the same page and accomplish the goals we had set before the season started. We made it through the evening and then the team went 8-1-2 to finish the season 9-9-4. Both ties were shootout victories in the playoffs, where we knocked off the number six and then the number three seeded teams. We won a regional championship and missed the state tournament by one game.

Lastly, there's the issue of competitiveness between boys and girls. Many coaches believe that boys are naturally more competitive than girls, which is true in some aspects. If you play small games in practice or have a fitness challenge, boys will compete to see who is the best. Sometimes a drill can become a competitive battle without any incentive from the coach, as boys are naturally more aggressive and want to exert their dominance. But girls are just as competitive in their own way; a coach just may have to bring it out of them. If you are conducting a drill where there are winners and losers, girls will sometimes go hard against their partner one round and then let the partner win the next. A coach might have to increase the incentive or place a bigger penalty on losing to bring out that intensity on a more consistent basis. Anson Dorrance has been successful at North Carolina in creating that environment every training session, understanding that with young women it is about the process and feeling of acceptance first. Once that is established, they can and will tear each other's hearts out in competition.

By treating young athletes with respect and allowing them to experience your passion for the game, regardless of their gender, they will respond. When I was coaching both genders in Wisconsin, many players asked which group I preferred, and I could never pick one over the other. Both genders bring different challenges and rewards and I enjoyed very positive experiences with my teams. Coaching both genders is not for everyone, but if your time allows and the opportunity presents itself, the rewards can be tremendous.

12 TEAM BUILDING

Team building is an essential component in any season of significance, and one that requires constant attention. It is not uncommon for extremely talented teams to fail to live up to expectations because players were not on the same page. Any team sport is made up of individual egos and, if left alone, the individual egos can prevent a team from reaching the full potential of the group. It is the coach's job to build team chemistry by creating an environment that allows for the individual elements of the team to mix together and form a cohesive bond. Early in the season, it is important to take off the coaching hat and put on the chemist mask. What can you, as the chemist, do to create a season of significance for your team, regardless of your record?

One recipe that you can cook up—both as a chemist and a chef—is pre-game pasta parties or dinners. My teams have routinely had pasta parties at a player's house before weekend tournaments and evenings before big games. If a dinner isn't scheduled or planned at a player's residence, the team may decide to meet at a local restaurant and eat together. Not only do these dinners provide a good chance for the team to hang out together outside of practice, but the pasta also fuels them for the upcoming contest. On occasion, though, these parties consist of an uneven pasta-to-cookie ratio. Even the best chemists can still have a sweet tooth!

When it comes to team building, the earlier, the better. In Wisconsin, the boys' season began before the school year, allowing for a period of time after the tryout process and before our first game of the season that we could use to strengthen our bond as a team. We used this period to stage an overnight boot camp, featuring fun outdoor activities that had nothing to do with soccer. When we started the boot camp, we had the opportunity to take it very literally. We traveled to a local army base and stayed in the barracks, utilizing their obstacle course, low ropes course, and their fitness center. We spent three days as a team away from parents, cell phones, and high school sweethearts, so that we had no choice but to get to know our team and their teammates. When, after two years, the army base became more active and this great opportunity had to be abandoned, we came up with our own version of the boot camp.

With the barracks no longer an option, my teams have instead gone on camping adventures, canoe trips, extended hotel stays, and school lock-ins, and gone paintballing and played laser tag. During these periods, our coaching staff carefully plans out the entire day with fitness challenges, soccer activities, entertainment, and many team-bonding exercises. Each year we try and do something a little different to keep it fresh and to keep our team motivated. In the event that costs are associated with these activities, we either hold a fundraiser or charge a nominal fee to cover the costs.

Many of my colleagues have gotten creative in looking for different ways to make team bonding a priority to start their seasons. One coach visits a local university and gets former players involved in a campus-wide scavenger event, culminating in a visit with the college coach and players. We usually end our initial team-bonding week with an alumni scrimmage, which provides some competition as well as a chance for the new crop of players to connect with the past. It also provides an opportunity for the coach to check in on former players and see how they have grown since leaving the program. If you build positive relationships with your players, alumni games are awesome events.

It is important to continue to plan activities during the season as well. My teams in the past have had a mix of nationalities and some teams have had a large hispanic representation. My wife and I hosted parties whenever the United States and Mexican national teams faced off, with each player bringing a Mexican or American dish to snack on. And, of course, at halftime we would fill a piñata, tie it to a tree in the yard, and bust it up (more sweets!).

Homecoming week is always a busy and distracting time for a high school team. Depending on the school, the week typically focuses on the football team, leaving the other sports at the school to take a back seat during the week. Our teams use this time to break from the mundane and have some fun ourselves. With games usually falling on both Tuesday and Thursday of homecoming week, our Wednesday practice is a light training day. For example, rather than hold a light practice, we planned a trip to the pool, not to swim laps, but rather to play what has since become an annual water polo match against the girls' swim team. This impromptu match became a great activity that promotes good team spirit during homecoming.

With distractions abounding at the conclusion of the week, we came up with a clever way to keep our players out of trouble after the football game on Friday night—holding an annual midnight practice that night. On a day when school let out early to hold a parade and other festivities prior to the football game, it is almost impossible to schedule a practice on that Friday. By holding a practice at midnight, our players are able to take part in the festivities prior to the game while limiting any nonschool sanctioned activities afterwards; they get a little toilet papering in, but not much more than that. And the novelty of a one-time practice under the lights makes for a cool setting that our players embrace. The downside is that it leaves my own house vulnerable to TPing, but you win some, you lose some.

Whenever you can find opportunities to strengthen the togetherness of your team, you should take them. These unique experiences will be cherished forever by players and coaches alike, even more than winning a tournament or achieving an individual milestone. Coaching, like life, is all about building relationships. Every day while interacting with players, students, and people within our working environments, we have the opportunity to build relationships. I want my players, my staff, and the faculty I work with to want to play for me, to want to work with me, and to want to attend our games because we have built meaningful relationships. Creating outings and events to strengthen these relationships goes a long way toward building a close-knit team, but ultimately relationships are built—and strengthened—every day. Every day is another opportunity for the chemist to help create a stronger bond. If you can build meaningful relationships with your players—and help them to build those relationships with each other—you will be on your way to having a season of significance.

13 OFF-FIELD CHOICES

It's great for coaches at any level to set goals and have personal ambitions, but at the end of the day it's important to remember that your main job is to enhance the experience of your players. At the high school level, all of your personal dreams and aspirations to turn a program around or win multiple championships are dependent on the performances of players ranging in age from fourteen to eighteen.

The players we coach love to play the game and spend a good amount of time honing their skills, but coaches need to always be aware that there is far more going on in their lives off the field. Each one of our players comes from a different background, has different goals in life, and has different aspirations of what he or she wants to accomplish on the field. At the same time, these young athletes are also dealing with the stress of academics, puberty, relationships, and their place in the strange world of high school. Good coaches are aware of and sensitive to the needs of their athletes on and off the field.

Many of the seasons you coach will be affected in some way by decisions your athletes make off the field. How do you handle these issues when they arise? What kind of messages do you send to your team regarding off-field behaviors? How often do you communicate with your players about these concerns and the possible consequences?

Some coaches choose to simply read the school rules aloud or pass out a document to the team and leave it at that. Some choose not to talk about alcohol and drugs at all and pretend there isn't or won't ever be a problem with substance abuse. But ignoring these issues does not mean they don't really exist. One coach I worked with told his players that alcohol and drug abuse was against the team rules and that he wanted them to avoid those behaviors. However, he would finish his lecture by telling those same players that if they did have a problem and were under the influence and possibly in need of help, they could call him and he would come and help them, no questions asked. What message did that coach send to his team by acting more like a buddy than an authority figure?

Most states have a governing body for athletics and require member schools to have an athletic code of conduct to address behavior and academic issues. Some states do not touch the substance portion, putting pressure on the coach to come up with his own plan. It is certainly advantageous to have a state- and school-wide plan that includes a team of attorneys to back up decisions and suspensions. If you are not that fortunate, you, as the coach, can come up with one your own, but you need to make sure your athletic director and principal will firmly back up your plan and your decisions.

A colleague of mine coached wrestling at our school, which had an athletic department code of conduct. He was worried about the behavior of his team away from the wrestling mat and one season decided to impose a stricter plan than what the school had implemented. He followed procedures and had the athletic director read and approve his plan. At his parent meeting prior to the start of the season, he had his players and parents sign the document, making sure they were all aware of the consequences.

As the season drew to a close, the team had an overnight tournament that required them to stay at a hotel close to the tournament site. As the coaches did a room check, they came upon three wrestlers who were under the influence of marijuana. The coach told them, as per their signed contract, that they were off the team. He called their parents and gave the information to the athletic director. When they returned to school the following Monday, the coach was called into the principal's office with the athletic director and was told that he had to reinstate the wrestlers. The principal and superintendent had buckled under parental pressure, causing a divide with the team and the coaching staff. One of the wrestlers was a senior with an outstanding record, and his parents came down hard on the district and the athletic director. Although the athletic director had approved the contract, he had to follow the orders of his superiors. The coach had done everything he was supposed to do, but his principal did not have his back and the wrestlers received no consequences for breaking their signed agreement. Feeling betrayed by his own district, the coach resigned after that season.

I would still recommend coming up with a plan and contract if there is none in place, but it is imperative that all superiors are on board. Follow whatever district procedures are in place and send copies of the contract to everyone, including the athletic director, principal, and superintendent. In other words, follow the CYA acronym: Cover Your Ass!

When I made the move to Florida, I had grown accustomed to working under an athletic code and was surprised to find that the state of Florida neither has nor requires one. I was hired the day before the boys' soccer season began and did not have all my normal procedures in place. I spoke to the team often about off-field behaviors and expectations, but after some early poor team performances I was made aware that a few of my players were coming to games high. I watched them closely the next game and although it was obvious that they were not in their normal state of mind, I had no proof that they were using and we had no code of conduct.

After the next practice I spoke with the three players involved individually and we had a conversation about the rumors, my observations, and team expectations. I did not accuse them, I just sent a very strong message about how situations like this would be handled going forward. Their attitudes changed, their play improved, and I learned that I needed to have my own set of standards instituted for the next season.

In the event that a player on your team makes a mistake or a poor decision off the field and a school or team suspension is handed down, how will you handle that player when the suspension is over? If that player was a starter prior to the suspension, will you put them right back in the starting lineup when it is over? How you handle this player during the suspension and immediately after the suspension will have a huge effect on the team going forward, and preferential treatment cannot be given to better players if the rest of the team is going to respect the code of conduct in place. The coach needs to walk the talk and hold all players equally accountable.

A suspended player is still a member of your team. The player will still be part of practice and the expectation will be for the player to compete in practice and help make his or her teammates better. Since the player is not eligible to play, their hierarchy in practice has changed, especially if that player was a starter and is no longer placed in the same grouping as the rest of the starters. Since that player is not suited up during games, it is best to find a different role during the contests, such as compiling game stats or assisting with equipment. These activities can serve as a small punishment for their behavior while at the same time keeping them engaged in the game.

When that player returns from the suspension, do you insert them right back into the starting lineup? Remember that the team has competed without that player in a number of games; rotations have changed, substitutions were affected. Other players, who have made the right choices off the field, have stepped up to compensate for the player's absence. While I personally think you send the wrong message to the team if the suspended player is immediately placed in the starting lineup upon return, whatever you do needs to be consistent with the expectations you have put in place.

I treat the situation in the same way that I would with an injured player. Once healthy and active, an injured player earns their time back on the field. I would not start them immediately on their return, but I would get them back in the rotation as soon as possible and wherever their ability puts them. I want the team to know that I give second chances and, once a player serves his or her penalty, they can expect to once again play an important role on the team. That being said, other players may have improved during the suspended player's absence and it is only fair to the rest of the players to expect that the returning player will earn that playing time back. As in everyday life, when you face a setback you have to prove yourself all over again. Nothing is given to you.

Coaches need to be prepared to have difficult conversations with their players. When rumors persist about the behaviors of players on the team—whether they come from the players, other students, faculty, or even parents—it is okay for you to have a conversation with your athletes and address the rumors or accusations. I have these conversations with another coach present (the double-up policy), and do not accuse the player but rather make them aware of what I've heard and what is being said about them. The message to that player is that if we are hearing these rumors, even if they are unsubstantiated, the player is probably putting themselves in positions that encourage the talk we are hearing. The player should reassess who they are hanging around with and what activities they are involved in.

Coaches may never know of the monumental impact they can have on the direction of a young person's behavior just by having a non-threatening conversation with them. If you are not comfortable with these potential confrontations, search for an assistant that possesses the skills that you do not have.

There will always be young players that make bad decisions, especially at the high school level when young kids are learning to become young adults. When a player makes a poor decision, be compassionate and be there for them, but don't let them off the hook. Help them learn from their mistakes, take steps to correct the behavior, and turn their negative into a positive. Use these mistakes as teachable moments and be there to help your players from repeating them in the future.

14 ONLY ONE STAT MATTERS

What would we ever do without statistics? We live in a statistic-driven world, and statistics measure the performance of our teams as well as our own performance as coaches. Stats are fun and can be motivating, helping coaches to compare past and present teams and players. But they can also be distracting and negatively affect a team's performances. It seems every year I have to have a chat with my teams about statistics and their importance—or lack thereof. We set statistics-based goals as a team (we want a winning season, we want a number of shutouts, we want a number of goals per game) to motivate our squads, but I'm careful not to highlight individual statistics so that our players do not get caught up in how many goals or assists they've recorded. Ultimately, only one stat matters: the W.

I keep individual statistics in a document that I do not share with the team until the end-of-season banquet, but I'm sure they know where they stand throughout the year by keeping track of their own accomplishments. Ask any player how many goals he or she has scored in a given season and you can bet more often than not that they'll know the number. By not sharing those stats with them, though, my attempt is to send a message that those personal statistics are not important to me, and any player concerned too much about individual statistics could become too focused on themselves and have a negative impact on our goals as a team.

Today's world of social media, team websites, and national tracking programs like MaxPreps ensures that all of that statistical information is at a player's fingertips at any given moment. In the NBA, the 2015-16 Golden State Warriors experienced many distractions as they pursued a team record that was never thought to be broken: winning 73 games in an 82-game season. It seemed impossible in the modern era, but they accomplished the feat because of their team-first attitude.

Early in the pursuit of the record, power forward Draymond Green was racking up triple-doubles at an impressive rate. The team was winning and through the course of his play the numbers and statistics kept falling into place. Green, a team player, was playing the role that the team needed him to play and, without deviating from his role, he was producing the numbers needed to produce the rare triple-doubles.

In a game the Warriors were clearly dominating, Green was on pace for another triple-double. With his team encouraging him, Green started to pursue yet another triple-double by focusing on only making the plays that would lead to that individual achievement. The course of the game changed and the team lost its flow because they were suddenly playing differently. They lost their big lead and almost let a game slip away despite having clearly dominated the contest. During his postgame media session, Green accepted responsibility for the team's loss of focus and acknowledged that it was because of his selfish play instead of his usual selfless play. The entire team had been working toward the same goal, but it was to get Green another triple-double rather than to win the game.

While Green, a professional, was able to own up to the incident, that is not always the case with high school athletes. It is important to have team discussions about statistics especially in the high school game where sportsmanship is supposed to be a cornerstone of the game. Coaches, too, sometimes forget the sportsmanship element.

It is great to see a player get their first goal and a team celebrate with that individual. There have been times in my career where, while on the losing end of a game, the opposing team subs in a rarely used player at forward near the end of the contest. This player is often one that doesn't play much or has never scored a varsity goal and his entire team tries to feed that player the ball and provide him with an opportunity to score. Sometimes the player is fortunate and scores on us, sometimes they are not. That team is having fun and we are not in a position to stop them. If that player scores, I celebrate with them.

However, when a team is up by a large margin—seven or so goals—at the end of the game, and a starting player on the opposing team has six or seven of those goals and the coach keeps them in the game to try and score goal number eight, sportsmanship becomes an issue. When the pursuit of individual statistics affects the team's performance or is contrary to the core values of the team, they become a distraction and a negative force.

While attending a coaching clinic, I had the opportunity to listen to an assistant coach of a professional indoor soccer team. The coach had a number of players fighting for playing time at the forward position and his group was lacking in production. The lack of production was resulting in few goals, and the losses were starting to pile up. That coach challenged his forward group to score a point every game in a point system in which goals were worth two points and assists one point. The forwards who produced the most points would receive more playing time, which meant more exposure and possibly a better contract. At the professional level, posting the stats and using them as a motivational tool improved production immediately.

At the time I thought, "Great, it worked for you, but I coach high school kids. I am not going to use that." However, few years later I found myself in a situation with six forwards who all thought they should be starting and earning more playing time. I pulled the group aside and told them that for the first four games of the season we would keep track of their stats, with each player receiving equal playing time. I was happy that I kept that little tool in my tool box, as the challenge worked. Two of the players rose to the challenge and increased their efforts, winning the starting positions.

We are in statistic-driven sport in a statistic-driven profession and I realize that my players have individual goals and dreams. We talk about their goals individually, and I will help them achieve those goals as long as we always keep what is best for the team in the forefront. I will keep a forward in a game to allow them to pursue a hat trick, but if the score is very one-sided in our favor that player will not be in the game. We do not sacrifice who we are and what our core values are so that a player can pad their statistics. If the team is successful, the individual accolades will fall into place. When players put themselves first the team suffers and individual accolades often suffer as well.

15 YOUTH PROGRAMS

The boys' high school soccer program in the Fond du Lac community enjoyed very little success from its beginning in 1986 through 1994. The first coach was there for nine years and was unable to produce a winning season during his tenure. The youth program in the community had started in 1974, was purely recreational, and had no long-range plan for growth or player development.

My soccer coaching experience began in 1989 when my wife and I signed Bart, our first-born child, up for this foreign sport. My soccer experience was limited to high school gym class and a college methods course on team sports. My soccer career began as a reluctant father taking on a coed recreational team of six-year-olds.

In 1989, the local soccer club needed to make significant improvements in order to make soccer a vital part of our community. I listened to many people express their displeasure, and these people of course had all the answers needed to turn things around. The trouble with complainers is that they fail to do anything to make change. Change requires effort, but they simply hope someone else does it. My belief is that if you are not willing to get involved, you have no right to complain. Instead of complaining or listening to the complaining, I decided to get involved.

A board spot opened for me in the fall of 1993. I left the room for a moment, came back, and found out I was the new club president by January of 1994. The positive was that not only did I become the president, we also had some new people elected to the board and there was a refreshed and enthusiastic group of soccer-minded people now in charge and ready to make change happen. Our enthusiasm mirrored the enthusiasm for soccer in America, and we were swept up in the soccer boom of the mid-90s. Our club exploded! In the years between 1994 and 2000, we increased our participation numbers from 300 players to 2,100. In 1994, we had two boys' select programs and no select opportunities for girls. By 2000, we had expanded to 130 recreational teams, 12 boys' select teams, and 11 girls' select teams.

The youth board focused on training coaches and making our program one of the top youth offerings in our community. As we focused on participation and player development, we saw a direct correlation to success at the high school level. The high school boys' program came under my direction in 1998 and, because of our great youth program, dedicated high school staff, and strong character values, we enjoyed a lot of success during my tenure, which ended in 2014.

As a coach at the high school level, your voice needs to be heard in the community. High school coaches may be the only people in the room that can bring an educational perspective to a group of club parents. High school programs require higher standards educationally and behaviorally, standards that are not necessarily part of a club program. During my time as a high school coach, I was able to have a huge impact on molding a club and a community.

When I moved to Florida, a whole new soccer world was opened up to me. Wisconsin youth soccer placed a significant emphasis on high school soccer, possibly due to the fact that so many high school coaches in Wisconsin were also club coaches at that time and therefore had a presence at the club level. Whatever the reason, it was clear that club soccer and high school soccer were on the same page. Florida, and much of the rest of the country, had moved away from such synergy, and battles between the two sides began to heat up.

I was hired to coach a very good high school girls' team in Florida, and prior to my tryouts I was caught off guard when four of my better players presented me with a letter from their club coach. This coach explained in the letter that his program was much better for these players than my recreational high school team. He laid out the girls' schedule, advising me when I would and would not have these players available for high school games and practices. When I brought this to my athletic director's attention, he could not believe the way the letter was written, but in the same breath told me that it is just the way it is. I did not believe my high school program should take a back seat to anyone, but it was my first season and I decided it was best to fight the battle by simply offering a superior program. It would ultimately be the players' decision.

I was also told when I took that position that this club issue would only involve the elite players on my team. The girls that played on the local competitive team were not a worry because the club was idle during the high school season. I came to find out that the local club had a director of coaching with a huge ego and a disdain for high school soccer. He started making things difficult for the rest of my players.

The problem wasn't the fact that I moved to a state where high school soccer seemed irrelevant, it was that young players were pulled in too many directions. Players were at two high-level practices two to three days a week when we didn't have a game. The weekends brought tournaments and showcases in which the players would play four to six games on a weekend. The players' health became a concern and at that point I had to have a conversation with the parents on my team. Someone has to start taking a stand for our young developing athletes. Too often, parents are not getting good information and money drives their decisions. They pay a lot of money for club experiences and judgments can become clouded.

Each and every coach will find themselves in different situations around the country. Some may be building a program in a community where involvement in an upstart club may be exactly what is needed for future success. The voice and guidance of an educator who coaches will help keep development on a path that will enhance player growth on and off the field. Some of you may be in areas where you are fighting a daily battle with clubs, premier leagues, and academies. Your role will be to provide the best program possible for players with many options.

It is easy to get mad and want to lash out at the competition. The best answer is to provide the better experience, show you care, and make your program bigger than the game. The players will see that and make the right choice when it comes to prioritizing their team choices. Personally, I am not concerned with what the club does. I make sure I treat my players with respect and provide opportunities that they can only get by being part of a high school team.

16 SELECTING A COACHING STAFF

It often saddens me to hear stories of how coaches are hired at many high schools around the country. Many are excellent coaches who would be successful at any level, including college or even professionally. They have chosen to stay at the high school level because they are educators and have a passion for teaching but also for developing young men and women. Sometimes, especially in soccer or sports that the school does not always prioritize, a warm body is hired to fill a position because the athletic director isn't a fan of the game or believes anyone can coach that sport. This impacts how people view that coach, and in many ways sets them up for failure. This is where a good parent group can help motivate or guide an athletic director to find a qualified candidate for the position.

In many high school programs, after conducting a thorough job search and selecting a qualified candidate who will be good for the kids and the program, the coach may inherit a staff they know nothing about. The staff could include a teacher who likes working with kids but doesn't know anything about the game, or one that just needed to pick up some extra cash. Whatever the scenario, the new head coach needs to focus on building relationships and developing expectations for the staff, while motivating the assistants to do more work than they may have signed up for.

If you are fortunate enough to hire or help select your own staff, look for loyalty and passion as the most valued characteristics. When I was hired for my first varsity head coach position, our junior varsity coach, Cory Clark, and I had already worked together for two seasons. We had already started to form a good relationship, and once I took over the program, that relationship turned into a great friendship. We possessed an attitude of gratitude as coaches. This program belonged to the community, not the coaches. We were fortunate to be able to put our stamp on it for a period of time. Clark was passionate and loyal and we agreed on our mission and the process—our program would be about doing things the right way.

When it was time to hire a new freshman coach, we did not get any applicants so we had to recruit our next freshman coach. One of our colleagues, Roy Ramirez was an outstanding art teacher who loved the game of soccer. He fit our loyalty requirement and was a passionate teacher; his soccer background included coaching his children at the recreational level but he had no coaching training. That did not deter us; we knew he was a good fit for our program and we could direct him to some good coaching courses.

© Vikki Winkler

It is easier to teach a new coach the game or a particular system than it is to change a personality. Finding a coach with a passion for working with young men and women and one who is concerned about the players as individuals and puts the program first should be a priority.

After working with the boys for many years, I had the chance to coach the girls' varsity team and found that I needed to correct a pattern that saw coaches come and go at the JV and freshman level every year. There was no stability within the coaching staff, therefore coaches did not develop a connection with the school or the program, and relationships were not being cultured. When I learned that two of the coaches would be moving on after the spring campaign I immediately recruited Clark and Ramirez from the boys' staff to come and help with the girls' program as well. Our relationship as a staff helped make our training, season planning, and soccer-related meetings much more enjoyable. Players aren't the only ones that can benefit from team-building activities.

I like to compare soccer coaches to the early settlers as they crossed the plains and found many unexpected problems in a dangerous new environment around them. Those early settlers often had to band together and circle the wagons to fend off attackers or the elements. As soccer coaches, we are still pioneers in our communities when it comes to promoting and selling our programs. It sometimes seems like there are other groups that want to attack our program and see us fail. Whether it is other athletic groups, parents, or the school administration, there will always be obstacles to overcome. Whatever the obstacle, the staff needs to band together, to support each other, and work as a team. If you inherit a staff, you need to develop trust which happens through good communication and showing support for each other at all times.

Trust is developed through integrity and following through on what you say you are going to do.

In smaller communities where soccer programs are in their infancy or which lack people with knowledge of the game, your options may be slim when a coaching vacancy opens. Sometimes the only candidate that surfaces is a parent of a player in your program. When considering a parent to be a member of your staff, you need to tread carefully.

Early in my career, I found myself in that exact situation. We needed a freshman coach and no school district employees expressed interest. Our next move was to open up the position to the public, and the only applicant was a father of one of the incoming freshman who also had a player on the varsity team.

In our program, all of the coaches are on the sidelines, schedules permitting, for the varsity contests. The JV and freshman coaches are there to help observe the match and serve as another set of eyes for the head coach. Their role is to observe and chat with players prior to a match or help assess their performance when they come off the field. Their role is not to shout instructions from the sidelines or have any communication with the referees. We have a one-voice policy and that voice belongs to the head coach.

This father candidate was very knowledgeable about the game and had coached some higher-level club teams that his children played for. He was familiar with all of the players in the program and, because he could bring something to the team with his knowledge and experience, we hired him. It wasn't long before we realized we had made a mistake. He had a hard time separating his role as a father from his role as a coach. In the first varsity tournament that we attended that fall, he coached from the sidelines and screamed at the officials. After almost getting me thrown out of the second match, I had to sit down with this father/coach and tell him he could no longer be on the varsity sideline.

This was very difficult for me as a young coach. He was respected in the community and he had a lot to offer, however he could not fill the role he was asked to fill when we hired him. This demotion caused other problems for us during that season. He was now back in the stands for varsity games, sitting with parents who were his friends from his years of coaching their children. Some coaches-only discussions that we had begun filtering back to the parents and causing dissension within the team. The trust we had worked so hard to gain as a staff was shattered.

We survived that season and learned a valuable lesson. We had to let him go after the season and search for a new freshman coach. This firing also severed a personal relationship that this parent and I had developed. Some coaches do a very good job coaching their own kids, but others cannot handle it appropriately. My recommendation would be to avoid putting a parent of one of your players on the staff, especially if they are not an educator.

Whenever there is a position to be filled on your staff, you need to make sure your athletic department is set up in a way that includes you in the hiring process. Make sure you do your research and check references for the candidate you are pursuing. Make sure to find someone who, when it is time to circle the wagons, will help watch your back.

If an assistant coach is lacking in the nuances of the game, there are great educational programs that you can steer them toward. Make sure you lay out the expectations you have for your staff and what the position will require of them. If they fit in your program, they will likely exceed any demands you put on them.

Other things to consider when hiring a new staff member are your own personal weaknesses. If your organizational skills are weak, maybe you can find an assistant to complement you in that aspect of the job and handle areas where you struggle. Look for an individual that can bring something to the team that you haven't been able to provide. Make your program better by bringing in good people to surround you.

The head coach is looked upon as the leader of the program. With young assistants, you will take on the role of a mentor. If they are interested in coaching for a long time, guide them and challenge them to eventually be prepared to take on a varsity program of their own. If they are happy and content to be a varsity assistant or junior-level coach, the goal is to keep them engaged and constantly gaining knowledge. For a great resource on helping develop leadership within your players and your staff, take some time to read Turn the Ship Around by L. David Marquet.

If you can give up some control and become a leader of leaders, allowing your staff to have input on training and player decisions, you will help them grow as coaches and strengthen your staff in the process.

17 BOOSTER CLUBS

What is your school district's policy on booster clubs? How are you providing support for your program's needs? General booster clubs that oversee all of the programs in an athletic department can be great if they are managed properly and fairly. Unfortunately, in my experiences, general booster clubs often look after the high-profile programs but neglect others, which often puts soccer on the back burner. I found it necessary to have a booster club that worked solely on the needs of our soccer programs. Booster club or not, it is necessary to get a parent group formed to help you with raising funds for your program. Your players deserve quality uniforms, balls, practice gear, portable goals, and other training equipment. School budgets cannot meet those needs in today's financial climate.

With the help of my parent clubs or booster clubs, we have been able to raise money for overnight stays, new uniforms, postseason awards, special t-shirts, game balls, promotional materials, coaches' education, and much more. Our parent group also puts together a media guide and a postseason yearbook that are unique to our programs.

It is important when establishing a booster club that the people involved understand that their activity doesn't extend to anything the team does on the field. Many parents will get involved with the expectation that their efforts will help gain favor for their son or daughter. It is important to take that off the table right away. I let parents know that while we need and appreciate their efforts, which will help the team and provide extra benefits for all of our athletes, they should not expect special treatment for their child.

One season, a talented underclassman made the varsity team, but there were two seniors in front of him earning most of the playing time. The player's father constantly asked what could be done for his child to earn more playing time. Following the chain of command mentioned earlier, I advised the father to have his child come and talk to me: it was a non-parent issue. Not satisfied with my answer, he asked, "If I got more involved with the booster club, would that help my son?" That ended our conversation but it also made me take a closer look at that perception and our new booster club. Many of the booster clubs in our community had a reputation for being very political. When we started one for soccer, we had to change a community-wide perception regarding booster clubs.

Several of the parents on my booster club had high-achieving players on the team. Their positions and playing time had nothing to do with the parents' efforts; the athletes earned everything they achieved. I continue to encourage parents to get involved because their efforts make every athlete's experience better, but they will not impact my decisions as a coach.

In another case of a parent misunderstanding her role in the booster club, we had a mom who worked as our treasurer for three seasons. She had an older child who had played for me, starting every game since his sophomore season. Her youngest son made the freshman team and then was a junior varsity player as a sophomore. In his junior year, he made the junior varsity once again and was passed over for varsity positions by a number of sophomores. When her youngest son did not make the varsity team that year, she left the booster club. Her son eventually quit the team, and she never spoke to me again.

It is understandable for her to give up her role on the booster club, but it was unfair of her to assume that her son would make a team because of the work that she did as treasurer. Her son had a lot of work to do to be a varsity-caliber player; his brother's success had given him a sense of entitlement and he failed to do what he needed to do to prepare himself. If you are in charge of a booster club, be aware that people that work hard for you may leave if things do not go their way. Just be ready to have someone around to help pick up the slack.

Many programs do not have booster clubs. Coaches find out they have very little to spend on their program and, when they ask their athletic directors for new equipment or supplies, they find out that fundraising for those needs is now part of their responsibility. If you want quality training equipment or new uniforms, you can get them—so long as you find the money on your own.

When I took my new position in Florida, that is exactly the situation I ran into. My program in Wisconsin had a great parent group and booster club and our players lacked for nothing. I took over a very successful program in Florida, and other than having an awesome locker room, we had no money. I knew that I needed to get parental support and start to get some financial help from that group. After the varsity team was picked, I made personal invitations for the parents of our varsity players and invited them for coffee in the school cafeteria.

I made a big pot of coffee, brought in donuts and pastries, and our parent group was formed. We had a great turnout and we were able to share ideas and plan out the special events we wanted for our team. We discussed our fundraisers and handed out responsibilities. That initial meeting helped the parents get to know me and it helped me understand a little more of the history of the program. We continued to have monthly meetings throughout the season.

Parents are willing to help and appreciate the chance to be part of their child's experience. The coach can take a proactive role and guide this group so that the needs of the group and team are met. A coach that can give up some control and allow the parent or booster group to help with the non-game-related activities will find more time to do what they're there for: coaching!

18 PARENT STORIES

An earlier chapter dealt with some parental issues and how to identify the different types of parents that you may encounter over your career. There will always be parents to deal with, and each and every one of them will have expectations of you, of your team, and of their child. Having guidelines and drawing some boundaries can help coaches handle parental issues with consistency. Still, no matter how much you prepare, you will face a challenge or two that you never saw coming. This chapter could also be titled, simply, Story Time.

I had a very strong player—a two-year starter, team captain, and senior—returning for her final season. She had a very vocal father who had been her coach as a youth player and could not put down his coach's whistle once his daughter moved on to the high school program. Our captains organized off-season indoor teams and they put teams together to play in local 3-v-3 tournaments. This captain put together a team and traveled to a local college that was hosting an open 3-v-3 event in which the team would play other high school girls but also compete against college players. There were no coaches and it was a chance for the kids to play and prepare for their upcoming spring season. The college players used it to maintain their touch and fitness during the off-season. After the event, I received a call from a college coach who was interested in my player and wanted to touch base. The coach told me that there was a parent in the gym, from our team, that had to be asked to leave. He was loud and obnoxious and continued to yell at the players and at the referees. I knew immediately who it was and I was concerned about the effect he might have on my team that upcoming season.

One of the tough parts of the coaching job is confronting behavior that has no place on your team or within your program. You can choose to ignore it and hope it goes away or you can confront the issue, understanding full well that if and when you confront the issue, you will more than likely have a disgruntled parent in your stands that will second-guess and arm-chair quarterback everything you do during the season. In this case, I chose to confront the parent head-on.

I asked to meet the parent and when I told him of the tournament complaint, he had no excuse for the behavior. He felt he was wrongly removed and did not see how his actions were in any way inappropriate. My message to him was that he had a pattern of this behavior and he often confuses his daughter during games because he is constantly coaching from the sidelines. We had a special team that year and we had a chance to do some great things on the field. My expectation for the parent was that he would discontinue coaching from the sidelines. He was welcome to come to the games and cheer for our team but at no time did I want to hear him yell instructions or yell at the referees.

To make sure he knew I was serious, I also told him that if at any time during the season I heard him doing either of those things, I would have the referee stop the game and have him removed from the stadium. Of course, I did not have that kind of power (especially with the referees), but he got the message and he knew that I meant business. The father was not able to attend many games that year because of a job promotion that required a lot of travel and kept him busy, but when he was there, I did not hear him.

Communication is key when dealing with student-athletes, the administration, and the parents of your players. Many complaints that coaches hear are that parents feel that some athletes on the team are favored over others. Maybe the coach invited some to an event but not others, or the coach had a few players stay and help with a younger team but not others.

It is important that you are as transparent as possible. Find a way to have a master calendar available to everyone and create a document that covers every aspect of your program as defined in an earlier chapter. Finally create an email list so you can be sure that every player and parent receives any communication you send. If they do not see the email or open the document, it is out of your hands. The information was provided and you did all you could to communicate with them.

At some point in your career you will probably get the dreaded anonymous letter. I have received a few over the course of my career. Some are quite comical, but most are hurtful. People that do not have the decency to ask a question or confront an issue face-to-face will still find a way to complain. Many parents fear that if they ask a question their child will get punished and playing time or team selection will be influenced. There are stories in every community where a parent questioned a coach and the child was kicked off the team or benched. These old wives' tales feed into the fear of a face-to-face meeting with the coach.

One season, I received an anonymous letter signed by the "soccer community." It told me who should play at what position, who should start, who should substitute in and at what point, and of course, which players should not even be on the team. I put that one in a file and didn't think about it for a month. As the team was preparing for our playoff run, a father approached me and apologized for sending the letter. His guilt had overtaken him and he told me he was just frustrated with his son's playing time early in the season. His son was an underclassman who eventually beat out a senior as the season progressed. The father was able to see the bigger picture and felt bad, eventually owning up to the letter. The "soccer community" ended up being a single frustrated parent.

But don't always expect an apology. Sometimes the letters attack you as a person, and the people writing them are not sending them to just you— sometimes they are also trying to discredit you in your community. You have to continue to walk the talk, keep things transparent, and always take the high road. It doesn't matter if you coach youth, middle school, high school, or beyond, you will eventually have a disgruntled parent send you a nasty-gram. I used to keep a file of these letters. Then one day I looked at them and decided I did not want to keep that negativity around. I put the entire file through the shredder.

My final story has to do with parental pressure on their child, a case of the tiger parent. Nothing is ever good enough for that parent and the player is grilled after games about their performance. Players who go home to another coach (their parent) dread these postgame conversations. One father came to me and was unhappy with his daughter's playing time. She had been playing soccer since age five and in her senior year was not a starter. He had put a lot of pressure on his daughter and she was playing with a fear of making mistakes, which inevitably led to more mistakes.

The father did not know that his daughter and I had many conversations about her role on the team and her willingness to accept that role. In order for my player to have a season of significance, the onus fell on me to have a conversation with the father. The conversation was about how his constant pressure was hurting his daughter's performance and how she was unable to enjoy the game and play without fear of constant correction at home. The father had been living through his daughter, hoping she would be the athlete he never was. It was ruining her soccer experience and destroying their relationship.

The player did not undergo a miraculous turnaround. It was too late in the season and my conversations with the father made no impact and we ceased communication. I ended up as the bad guy in the father's story, but trying to provide the best experience for the player and getting the most out of her for our team took precedence over the relationship I had with the parent. Not everyone will be comfortable with family situations, and getting a counselor from the school involved may be another option. In the end, you have to do what you feel comfortable doing and, when you can't, find someone who can.

A few coaching rules to remember when dealing with parental issues:

- **Double up.** Always have another coach or adult present when having difficult conversations with a player or parent.
- **Give it 24 hours.** Wait 24 hours before calling back a disgruntled parent or responding to a nasty email. It is always better to let your emotions settle before dealing with potential conflict.
- **Bus rides are important.** Make it mandatory for your players to ride the bus home from contests whenever possible. This keeps them away from the arm-chair quarterback in the family vehicle after a contest.

As your career extends, the stories will pile up. Keep your integrity in check and always do what you say you are going to do. Communicate as much as possible and get your messages out in as many ways as possible. Lastly, stay consistent. When parents begin to realize that you always have the same response to the same questions they will stop asking them and allow you your space to coach. As soon as you give in to one parent, you will open the floodgates, and once that happens, you better have a big boat!

19 FRIENDS

A yellow card means "Warning!" Take caution and consider your actions so the behavior isn't repeated. I am using the yellow card to warn you about friendships.

Once you become a head coach you control playing time, roster spots, and the level at which a player will be placed. Parents who did not know who you were before are now showing an intense interest in you. They want to help out or even possibly strike up a friendship, hoping that you will treat their child favorably down the road. I am not telling you not to make new friends; this is just a yellow card, a warning.

My wife and I have met many great people through soccer. The sport served as something that we had in common and our friendships were strengthened because of the game. On the flip side, however, we have lost many friends or had many friends drift away because they were unhappy with their child's placement on a team.

When I took over the girls' program a father came up and congratulated me on the position. I had worked with his daughter at some youth camps and she was still a couple years away from entering the high school. This father went on to say that he was disappointed the previous coach had stepped down because he had been sucking up to him for four years. He had never spoken to me during that time. He stated out loud what many people think, but would never admit to.

My wife and I were introduced to a nice couple with some young kids a few years ago and we developed a good relationship. My wife, who had been burned before, jokingly told the couple that if their kids played soccer we probably could not be friends. The couple said not to worry; their children were just recreational level players and they knew their kids had to make it on their own. It was a good friendship until four years later, when their son did not make the varsity team as a sophomore. The player did not belong on the varsity team, which was clear to everyone but his parents. They drifted away and no longer communicated with us, apparently forgetting about the "making it on their own" comment.

Early in my high school coaching career I still taught at the middle school level. My wife and I had some friends whose children were younger, one of whom was a student of mine at the middle school. One afternoon while leaving school, I found the student smoking in the bushes on school grounds. After taking the young man to the principal and calling home about the incident, the parents started to distance themselves from our relationship.

These parents had always told me to watch out for the child; if I saw anything of concern I should share that with them so they could address it. In this case, I had no choice but to take the student to the principal. The family was embarrassed and ashamed about the behavior and let a middle schooler's mistake ruin our relationship.

Just like a yellow card, this is just a little reminder to tread lightly when new friends pop into the picture. If their children play the sport you coach, there could be ulterior motives.

20 FACULTY, ADMINISTRATION, AND THE SCHOOL COMMUNITY

If you are a high school coach, you have probably run into faculty and administration that may not even know your school has a team. At almost every soccer game I have attended, whether at my home field or on the road, there are very few school staff attending the games. Most have never experienced a soccer match. And unless that member of the school staff has had a child of their own in the program, they might not even know when the soccer season takes place.

If you talk to athletic directors, soccer is considered a second- or even third-tier sport in many of the athletic programs. This secondary status carries over to budgets, pep rallies, and school announcements. Many soccer coaches have stories of how they had to start their programs by offering a club and showing the local school board that there was enough interest in the sport. Athletic directors may remember having to deal with pushy parents as these programs fought for existence and still hold a grudge against the sport many years later. When athletic directors hear the word *soccer*, many immediately think of our beautiful game as a pain in their beautiful derrieres.

Implementing a core values program and getting your team to buy into it will help your players be better citizens in their school. It will not be long before your student-athletes will be known as the soccer team. If there is an incident regarding a player that made a poor choice, it is immediately seen as a reflection of your program. When teachers reach out to me about a student's behavior, they always label them as "your player." They refer to the student-athletes as if they were my own children.

It has been said that players start to take on the characteristics of their coach. If a coach is arrogant and controlling, the players start to project that same attitude in school and in games. Players have to be reminded constantly about representing your program, whether they are in school, at home, or in the community. If you are walking the talk and teaching character, your players will be great representatives for the program.

Communication between your program, the athletic department, administration, and faculty needs to be a priority. When you host special events make sure you send invitations to the entire staff and let them know you would really like to see them at your games. The communications should also include any community service your team performs or special recognition your team earns. The National Soccer Coaches Association of America (NSCAA) hands out many awards for high school teams that are released throughout the year.

We have been fortunate to receive several academic awards through the NSCAA, which emphasize the student-athlete aspect of high school sports. We make sure we take a picture and send a press release to the local paper so that our community—and more importantly our school community—recognizes our players for more than their talent on the field. The NSCAA has individual student-athlete awards and team ethics awards and it is important to share those achievements with your school community and administration to give them a better, more well-rounded representation of your team.

I am always challenging players to be ambassadors for our sport and our program. With a strong core value program, your players become extensions of you, the coach. When they start walking the talk of the program, faculty and staff start to recognize that your team carries themselves differently. When they become model students, it is the best advertisement possible for your program.

We have tried many different ways to get our faculty and administration to attend our contests, which is a battle regardless of the sport. We came up with a great way to involve teachers in our games, and this little addition to your schedule will provide more goodwill for your program than almost any other thing you can do. The faculty in your building will brag about your program once you hold your first Teacher Appreciation Night.

We host an annual Teacher Appreciation Night with our boys' team in the fall and then repeat the event with the girls in the spring, selecting one home game during the season and designating it Teacher Appreciation Night. Each varsity player selects a teacher that they want to thank or recognize for making a difference in their education. The players are allowed to pick an elementary, middle school, or high school teacher. If they are on the varsity team for multiple seasons, we encourage them to select a different teacher each season.

The players give me their teacher's name and I create an invitation. The players then present the invitation to the teacher and inform them of the event. The teachers are given the date and time, and they are asked to provide me with a t-shirt size. We make a special event t-shirt with the player's name and number on the back, or we solicit sponsors and put their logos on the back of the shirt.

We create a special program and provide a ticket for the teacher and a guest, and our concession stand provides them with a drink and popcorn for the game. I have each of the players write a personal thank you note to their teacher that they give me to hold until the game. At halftime, we call the teachers to the field and recognize them with the player. We take a photo and the teacher is given the letter as they walk onto the field. Our soccer parent group or booster club provides a reception following the contest.

The teachers are always excited for this game. The administration allows the teachers to wear the event t-shirt to school on game day and they walk around like they won a Teacher of the Year award. Elementary teachers are floored when a high school player remembers them and they are chosen. This program was adopted by almost every other sport at our high school. The athletes get excited about it and take the enthusiasm to their other sports. I have shared this promotional tool with many coaches over the years with great reviews and it never fails to make a strong connection with the school faculty and administration.

The not-so-pleasant part about dealing with administration is when you have to lobby for equipment, equal playing facilities, and equal or fair funding from the school budget or general booster clubs. It can be challenging to advocate for your needs when money is tight especially when another coach is denied a similar request. I have seen the squeaky wheel get the grease on more than one occasion when other coaches had a greater need. When you squeak for everything, you become annoying and soon will be tuned out. I recommend you choose your battles wisely. Make sure what you are fighting for is worth the struggle.

You may not get what you want immediately, but when people start to observe your players and see the character start to ooze from your program, they will want to get on board. Continue to promote your student-athletes and the great things they accomplish both on the field and off at every opportunity, and you will enhance your team's perception among the administration and community at large.

21 USING A PLAYER JOURNAL

You may or may not use a coaching journal—a daily or weekly record of the activities, practice plans, player meetings, and general thoughts—as your season progresses. This is an area that has been hit or miss for me; I often start one at the beginning of the season and my best intentions of keeping up with it often slide. As I look back over my career, I wish I had done a better job of journaling so that I could relive some of the great memories of the past. That being said, having your players keep a journal is something you should seriously consider.

If you are thinking that I am suggesting more work for you to do, you are correct. However it is a good practice to get into and can help you discover potential issues with your team before they develop into problems. To start, provide each player with a notebook and a pen in a gallon-sized Ziplock baggie. This allows them to keep the journal in their bag and have access to it throughout the season. I give the players prompts to write about and I collect them either weekly or bi-weekly, read them, and return them to the players the following Monday.

Upon receiving the notebook, their first prompt is to write a letter to themselves. I instruct them to be honest with themselves about what they expect for the season and write down what they think their strengths and weaknesses are and how they will use them or improve on them. I then ask them to write a description of what they have done to prepare for the upcoming season and how they think tryouts will go for them. During the tryout process, I expect them to write about their experiences and their efforts every day. At the conclusion of the tryout I ask them to tell me how they think the season will go and to share with me their personal goals for the season. The players are told the journal is like a soccer diary that only I will read; it is not something that they need to share with anyone else unless they want to. I explain the journal to parents at the parent meeting and let them know that this is a personal log for their athlete.

We designate the last 30 pages of the journal for game evaluations. After each contest, they are to do a post-match analysis of their performance, the team's performance, any tactics that the other team did well, and which players on the opposing team stood out. These become very valuable assessments in the event that we see the same team later in a conference tournament or playoff game. They can include information about their pregame meal, their recent work or class schedule, or anything else that may have had an effect on their performance. These player reponses are great to read and they help improve the player's soccer IQ. They start to evaluate individual and team performances with a higher level of thinking.

As part of our character development with our program, we introduced a word of the week throughout the season. If we talk about resiliency, we give the team a picture of what resiliency looks like. We have the players put the word in their journal and then give an example of a time they witnessed that character trait in action. They can use a team example or an example from another sport or a game they may have watched.

When the journals are collected each week, I read them all over the weekend and write a response or a note to each player. These responses are usually words of encouragement or an answer to a question the player had. Sometimes players will write a question they have instead of addressing me face-to-face. Teenagers are not always eager for face-to-face confrontations and this gives them another avenue to express a thought or concern. If it is something that needs to be addressed in person, I will seek out that athlete. There are occasions where something is amiss with the team and the concern is brought to my attention. For example, one year a few of the players were picking on one of the underclassmen on the JV team. The player being picked on was not confident enough to address his teammates, so it was written in the journal. Our staff was able to handle the issue without calling out a player or making the scene uncomfortable. We were able to take care of a concern that could have been a huge distraction later in the season.

If you are proficient with computers, you can do many journal activities in a web-based program. One of my coaching colleagues, John Ziperski, uses Google forms for his journaling activities. He gets immediate postgame feedback and the responses are only seen by him. Coach Ziperski does this with his girls' team and, because it is online, there is no chance someone else will look in the player's journal. If you do not have the time or tech savvy to accomplish this, you may have an assistant help with those skills.

The journal is a personal record of the season and is something the player can save and look back on when the memories start to fade. It is also a great tool during the season. What a player ate prior to a great game or what kind of outside stressors impacted a poor performance are valuable pieces of information to document. There are many ways to utilize a journal for personal and team performance, and while it may require a little more time, a journal can be a very valuable tool throughout the course of a season.

22 THE OTHER COACHES

Every coach would love for their athletes to devote the majority of their time to the sport they are coaching. When I taught at a small school—one in which athletics, band, chorus, and theatre all had to work together and share students—communication was outstanding and crucial for the success of those programs. Teachers and coaches worked together and schedules were made to provide the student-athlete the opportunity to be involved wherever they had an interest. In the larger school environment this isn't always the case. Many program advisors and coaches become very possessive of their participants and force students to choose one activity over the other.

Some coaches believe that if the athlete isn't 100% committed to their sport—in season and off—the team will not be as successful. I have seen band directors create tougher schedules than any athletic team, making it impossible for those students to pursue activities other than band. Students do not want to let their mentors down and they struggle with these decisions because they love the activities they are involved in and enjoy being with the teacher or coach in charge of that activity. They often have internal struggles because they are afraid of disappointing a teacher or coach.

Students are going to pursue what they enjoy, but if we put too many restrictions or demands on their time, they may choose to pursue a different sport or activity. If coaches take the attitude that it is a privilege to be in the position we hold and a privilege to work with these young men and women, it will help in dealing with the curious athlete, one that wants to explore multiple opportunities.

It is when coaches begin to think we are bigger than the program, bigger than the school itself, that we set ourselves up for conflict. I have dealt with coaches who look at the athletes in their programs as possessions. When an athlete chooses to leave their program for another sport or activity, the coach becomes angry and distances themselves from that student. I have had experiences where coaches sever relationships with other coaches because of a choice a student-athlete made. The student will only be in your program for a few years; it is not worth letting the choice of one student-athlete ruin a professional relationship that may span a career.

I was a freshman high school football coach prior to accepting the head soccer position and both sports were played in the fall. We had just hired a new football coach and I was part of that new coach's football program. I was eager to learn and helped develop many good players that excelled at the varsity level. My path on the gridiron staff was to move up to the junior varsity level or take on an assistant role with the varsity team. We had good coaching chemistry and there was mutual respect between all members of the staff.

When my coaching path changed and I decided to pursue soccer, I was shunned by the staff I had spent the past five years with. Instead of being happy that I was going to pursue my passion, my colleagues took it as a personal betrayal. I was now a threat to their program. Many freshmen played soccer in the off-season and football in the fall. With my change of high school coaching responsibilities, some of those players decided to continue with high school soccer due to the relationships we had developed.

The head coach of the football program started harassing the players that left his program. It began as friendly banter about wanting the player back on the football field but escalated to badgering them about why they quit. It became such a problem that I addressed the head football coach face-to-face, though that meeting did not help and, if anything, created more problems and a bigger divide. We eventually had a meeting with the athletic director and the football coach was put on notice.

This was a man that I respected and had worked closely with. He let his fears and the belief that he owned these players affect the way he went about his daily business. We continued to work in the same building for another decade with no communication between us. The attitude of the head coach of the biggest program in our school affected the school environment for years, even after he left. There was a soccer versus football rivalry in our school that still exists today.

On the flip side, girls' soccer and girls' track were two competing sports in the spring. Many of the female athletes ran track and played club soccer in middle school. These athletes would excel in the sport of their choosing when they arrived at the high school level. Athletes could only pick one team to participate in, so many soccer girls chose track in high school and many track athletes chose soccer.

The head girls' track coach and I were colleagues in our teaching assignments and even coached track together years before I took on the girls' soccer position. Our relationship was totally different than the one I had with the football coach. We both realized that students will simply choose what they like better; it was not a popularity contest between the two of us. Many of his track girls still played competitive soccer in the off-season. We planned off-season workouts for female athletes and shared weight room supervision duties. We both had successful programs and took pride in the successes of every girl involved in a spring sport.

I am a huge proponent of multi-sport athletes and the value of high school athletics. I work to build relationships with all of the coaches in the building, especially those that have programs in my off-season. In the winter, our school offers swimming, a high-endurance sport that does not fall during soccer season for boys or girls. I encourage players to swim because it helps increase their cardiovascular system and gets them off their legs for awhile. I encourage my players to run track and my goalkeepers to pursue basketball. Whenever we have a goalkeeper drought looming in our future, I look for young basketball players to see if they are interested in soccer.

When you read stories about professional athletes, regardless of the sport, you find that many of them were multi-sport athletes. Specialization is taking many young athletes out of our programs. Seventy percent of our youth athletes quit sports before the age of 14, before they even enter high school programs. Many have been pressured to pursue one sport as early as elementary school. When they lose interest or don't develop fast enough, they leave sports altogether. If they had a wider base of sports and activities, they could possibly be successful in another area. Coaches have to do a better job of working together and allowing athletes flexibility to experience more opportunities.

If you have great relationships with the other high school coaches in your program, the next hurdle will be with a club team. Clubs can become a huge pain in your side and put your program in jeopardy.

Depending on the state you are in, you may be battling a different club sport during your season, or even the same club sport.

The problem with dual participation arises with training, rest, and recovery. In Florida, we had no practices or competitions on the weekend due to club conflicts. There were nights when players had a high school practice and then traveled an hour for a club practice. There were even nights when players would travel to club practice after school and show up later for a high school game. Add three to five games over the weekend and players did not have any time to rest, let alone do homework or keep up with classes. At one point in my season, the girls had 28 straight days of training and games.

This was unacceptable and I had to have a parent meeting to address my concerns for these young athletes. Ultimately, it ended up in the hands of the parents, who stood up to the club coach and, at least locally, forced a change. Clubs are operated based on how much money they can bring in; the best interest of the athlete is not always their primary concern. It is neither possible nor advisable for a coach to try and control what a player does on their own time, however educating players and parents about rest and recovery are within your control.

Club coaches, too, tend to come and go. The relationships to focus on are your coaching colleagues at your school or university. These people are fighting the same battles as you. The more you communicate and work together, the greater success will come to your players and, ultimately, your entire athletic department.

23 OFFICIALS OR, ARE YOU BLIND?!

If you are an official reading this, I am surprised. According to sports fans, the rumor is that most officials are blind. Every coach has dealt with officials both good and bad. Much like our players, officials have good and bad performances. Most officials love the game and officiating is their way of staying involved. It may be hard to fathom, but officials are people, too.

To get a better appreciation for officials, I would recommend becoming one. I spent twenty years officiating soccer and wrestling. It was not only a great way to earn a little cash, but it also allowed me to develop techniques for dealing with conflict. Similar to coaching, there are people that love your decisions and those that find fault with those same decisions. It is impossible to make everyone happy when you are the one managing the contest.

I used the word *manage* here because far too many officials try and control the match, meaning they feel that they are in charge of the outcome and become part of the game. The officials that I have had issues with in my career were the ones that needed to be the center of attention. The officials that do the best job are the ones you do not even know are on the pitch. As a referee instructor for a brief time, we told our young referees to try and manage games by communicating with the players (e.g., warning them prior to a card). As a coach, I appreciate the referee that lets me know a player is about to be carded. I, in turn, remove that player from the contest and have them settle down before I put them back on the field.

The demonstrative referees, the ones who like involving themselves in confrontations with a coach or even a player, are the referees that need to rethink why they took up this profession or hobby. Many referees are former players or coaches who just want to give back to the game, and coaches should have an attitude of gratitude when working with officials so they feel appreciated and continue honing their craft. Ultimately, without officials we cannot play the game.

My experience as an assistant athletic director provided me the opportunity to watch hundreds of contests involving a variety of sports. It amazes me to continually see officials get verbally abused by players, coaches, and especially fans. It is embarrassing to represent a school whose fans treat the officials with so much disrespect. In contests like football and soccer, the fields are bigger and offer a degree of separation from the fans. Basketball and wrestling bring out the worst in people as the fans are usually closer to the action. Basketball officials always amaze me with their self-control and their ability to ignore the crowd.

As a young varsity soccer coach, I was dismayed by what some of my coaching counterparts would say to our game officials. What alarmed me even more was how often the referee took the verbal abuse. These coaches not only argued the calls, but would often use inappropriate language and even call out the official by name. What was even more difficult for me to understand was how veteran coaches were given a lot of slack when questioning the referee while I, being a first- or second-year coach, would ask for a clarification and be told to keep my mouth shut.

Throughout my coaching career, I have seen high school coaches work the official. I understand that with some sports it is an accepted practice and part of the game, basketball coaches being an example of that. I look at working an official as a gamesmanship tactic and an example of poor sportsmanship in the game of soccer, which is a game for the players. Constantly chattering to the official to try and influence an outcome should not be accepted or tolerated.

The coach should allow the team captains the responsibility of talking to the officials. Choose captains who can represent you, the coach, on the field. Train these young men and women how to respectfully deal with the officials throughout the course of the game. This fosters the development of your players' ability to grow and learn how to address authority in heated situations.

It is a rare occurrence for me to question a referee's decision once the game is over. I may ask for clarification during the contest or I may ask to speak to the official at halftime, but once the game is over, I simply let it go. If I see the official at a meeting or in a tournament at a later date and I remember a situation or a call, I may ask them about it since the heat of the moment has passed; chances are, though, that I will not even remember. I am sure there have been games where I made a fool of myself yelling about a call that a few days later I will have totally forgotten about. I make a conscious effort to remain calm and let the players handle the in-game situations.

When I speak to the team about respect as one of our core values, this is where I reinforce behavior towards officials. Our team will respect the game and the men and women who choose to officiate our contests. We take that attitude of gratitude when it comes to dealing with officials, understanding full well that without their service we would not be playing the game. My players can either deal respectfully with officials on the field or find themselves removed from the game, and no one is allowed to scream at an official from the bench.

It is especially important for my freshman and JV coaches to be tolerant of the officials in their games. Like coaches at the youth level, these games often have rookie officials that are going through a learning curve, and many have minimal experience as referees. Some have a playing background, but some will have only recently picked up the game. Yelling at them and constantly correcting them will send them running away from the game. My sons were all referees at some point in their lives. One of them was a seasoned youth referee and started to referee high school JV games as a twenty-year-old college student. My son, Brett, and I were reffing a JV high school tournament together and he made a close offside call. Brett was in the right position and he made the right call. The coach whom the call went against went ballistic on the sideline and continued to harass Brett through halftime and after the game, even following him to the referee tent after the game. It was not a positive experience for Brett. He dealt with the coach and handled himself well for a young referee, but that confrontation caused him to decide to discontinue his reffing hobby. There were plenty of other part-time jobs available for a college kid that didn't involve such negative experiences.

We should remember that we set the tone for treatment of officials by the way we talk to them and react to calls. Our teams will behave the way we behave. Reflect on your most recent actions and behavior with a referee. Did your behavior match your message? There will always be calls we do not agree with and referees with whom we will not get along. Regardless of how blind that official appears to be, most of them are doing this as a way to give back to the game—and their eyesight is just fine.

If you are a referee, try to manage your matches without becoming the center of attention. Keep yourself fit enough that you can be close to the play. Nothing bothers soccer coaches and players more than an official who doesn't leave the center circle.

I would recommend that every coach spend a little time with the official's shirt on. Building relationships with officials is just as important as building relationships with players, parents, staff, and administrators. They are part of your coaching world, and chances are you will see them many times over the course of your career.

24 PREPARING YOUR TEAM

How often have you found yourself trying to get your team to perform a specific task during a game? You are yelling from the sideline to overlap on the wing or make diagonal runs into the box and nothing resembling those actions is taking place on the field. During your halftime speech you describe opportunities to attack or ways that you can reinforce your defense and you tell the players what to do. However, when they go out for the second half, nothing even remotely close to what you told them is happening on the pitch.

I have witnessed and listened to many coaches shouting instructions to their teams and becoming very frustrated as their instructions are not executed. As the coach grows more and more frustrated with the team, the coach screams louder and pulls players off the field, giving others an opportunity only to get the same results.

Often what the coach fails to realize is that all this great knowledge that is spewing out of his mouth was not first executed in practice. The tactical advice the coach gave was correct, and if the team had been able to execute it there may have been favorable results. Instead, the team did not understand the directions. Often a coach will make a tactical correction at halftime and every player nods in agreement. The coach thinks the team is good to go, yet the tactic is never performed. The players never worked on what the coach wanted with this particular team. Players may have done something similar on a club team or some other team they once played on, so they thought they knew what the coach wanted, but not everyone was on the same page.

This is where putting a daily practice plan and a seasonal practice plan together prior to the beginning of the season comes in handy. Before the start of your season, determine what system you want to run, what attacking patterns you want to emphasize, and how you will defend. Think about your set pieces, how you'll play when you are ahead, and how you'll play when you're behind. What happens if you have to play a man down, or you are beating a team by a huge margin? All of these scenarios need to be practiced.

A good example of this happened in my first year at Ida Baker in Florida. We knew we were playing an evenly matched team and we worked on a corner play to perform late in the game if we had a lead. If we were up by one with five minutes to play, we would yell "Baker!" and dribble to the corner. We stressed in practice that we will not try to score on this play, but rather stall in the corner and keep the ball in the attacking third. Sure enough, the situation presented itself, but we had a forward in the game that was not at the practice when we drilled the tactic. With two minutes to play that forward had a breakaway opportunity and was looking for personal glory and went to goal. He lost the ball, the opponent countered and we left the contest with a tie. Despite the fact that we went over the tactic again prior to the game, the player never drilled it and therefore he did what he thought was correct: he tried to score.

Regardless of how well you prepare your team, even if you think you have covered every possible scenario, there still may be a game situation that you find yourself unprepared for. You hope in those situations that your training and your character education will help the team prevail. Let me give you an example of something you would never think you would ever have to experience.

In 2004, I had an unbelievable team. I had coached the bulk of this group from the time they started select as ten-year olds until they were fourteen. By the time these players were seniors in high school, there was no situation on the soccer field that they hadn't seen or that we hadn't trained for. As their coach that season, I prepared the training and made substitutions but this team was on a mission and they took responsibility for the season. The boys put together an undefeated conference season and went into the playoffs that year as the top seed in the sectional.

The team cruised through the playoffs and qualified for the first boys' state soccer tournament in school history. In the state quarterfinal, we scored early and led 1-0 for nearly the entire match. As the clock counted up to 80 minutes and the horn sounded, one of the opposing players fired a long shot at the net. Hearing the horn and understanding that in soccer the ball is dead where it is when time expires, we started celebrating as that shot went in the net. The assistant referee, looking to make himself part of the game, ruled it a goal. The center referee had ruled the game over but allowed himself to be swayed by the assistant and sent the game to overtime.

My goalkeeper was furious and mentally out of the game at this point. We were aware of his temper and his teammates controlled the match and did not allow a shot on goal during overtime, sending the game to penalty kicks. In the penalty kick shootout, our goalkeeper had regained his composure and was stellar, saving the first three shots as we buried ours and sent our team into our first state semifinal.

The team was staying at a nice hotel about 25 minutes from the state tournament site. Every minute of our entire experience was plotted out ahead of time: where and when we would go to dinner, when they could use the pool, the team meeting before curfew, wake-up call, team breakfast, and so on. The players knew what the agenda was and how we were going to prepare ourselves for our game the next evening. Everything was going according to our preseason plan.

That is when our best laid plans went south. The team had settled in for curfew and our final checks were made for the night. My coaches and I had adjoining rooms and my wife, our team photographer, was along for the event. The coaches had turned in and my wife, Vikki, was running back and forth to the laundry room late into the evening so the team looked sharp for the semifinal. Her uniform cleaning was completed around one in the morning and we had just turned in for the evening. At 2 a.m., a fire alarm went off. We planned on staying in the room but a player called me and said they looked out their room and saw a police officer. Since I was responsible for 24 young men and an entire coaching staff, I ventured down to the front desk to see if we needed to do anything.

As I approached the desk I observed an undercover police officer crouched with his revolver drawn. As I entered the lobby I was whisked away to a conference room with ten other people. It was the same conference room we were meeting in for breakfast later that morning. That is when I learned what was happening.

A guest on the floor above us had murdered his girlfriend earlier that night, while we were in our quarterfinal game. He had shot her seventeen times with an AK-47. No one had heard this happen and she was dead in his tub. At 2 a.m., feeling remorseful, this man had pulled the fire alarm. When the guest next to his room looked out, he shot the man in the head. He then sprayed another forty plus rounds down the hallway. Another guest looked out her door and shut it quickly; he sprayed the door with bullets and wounded that guest. This man had murdered two people and wounded two others. He ran out of ammo, but intended to get more and continue his shooting spree. Fortunately the police and then a SWAT team arrived and ended the situation.

As the SWAT team was clearing the hotel and securing the shooter, I was in a conference room with strangers four and a half hours. I communicated with my wife by cell phone but did not want to disturb the players or my coaches, or contact parents until things were clear and we had more information. The media had started to surround the hotel and the story would be live on news channels throughout the state; I needed to contact parents and let them know our team was safe and unharmed. It was a helpless feeling sitting in the conference room waiting for the event to end. At 6:00 a.m., I was allowed to contact parents. My wife had been handling some calls from our room.

The SWAT team received some misinformation that there were two shooters involved, so at 5:30 a.m. they went on a room-to-room clearing procedure. The players woke up to two SWAT members going through their rooms with assault rifles scanning every inch of the room for another gunman. Needless to say the team was a little shaken and my macho high school boys were frightened after learning of the evening events. After this, the players flipped on their TVs and saw the exterior of our hotel on the morning news.

I returned to my room at 7:00 a.m. We had scheduled a team meeting and breakfast at 10:00 a.m., in the same room where I had just spent the night. We wanted to try and stay on schedule, but the boys had another shocking experience when they shuffled into our meeting room. Two body bags were taken out of the hotel right in front of them.

This was not something anyone plans for. We were ready for just about anything that season, but not this. We changed our plans and went to a matinee showing of *The Incredibles*. We had to get away from the large media pool that swarmed the hotel. Clearly, the team was emotionally shaken by the event, and we asked the state association if we could postpone the game for a day. The state association had no contingency plan and ruled that games were to be played regardless.

While we tried to maintain some normalcy, we were shuffled in the back way at the stadium. The organizers were trying to avoid making our game a media circus. Everything they made us do disrupted our normal routine and we were not prepared for a match of that caliber. We were not ready for the game and gave up a goal within the first three minutes. We battled hard but our team was physically and emotionally drained from the previous night's events. We gave up a penalty kick near the end of the contest and lost 2-0 to end our year with a record of 26-1-2. It was the best season in program history, but short of our goal.

Fortunately, because of the great communication within our team and with our parents, we were able to get the message to everyone that our players were safe. Our team learned that there will always be more important things in life than the result of an athletic contest.

We stress to our teams to worry about the things they can control: preparation, effort, and attitude. The rest will take care of itself. The more prepared you are, the easier it will be to coach and communicate what you are teaching, but as we found out, there are always situations beyond your control.

25 RULES AND THE REASONS FOR THEM

The game of soccer doesn't have rules, rather it is governed by the laws of the game. The high school association has turned those laws into an extensive rulebook that we have to follow. If you are in any state other than Florida, you also have an athletic code that is full of rules ranging from school attendance to substance abuse. While rules are necessary, they can become an administrative nightmare. The more rules you pile on, the more potential problems you may have to address. I certainly have my own team rules and, coaching in Florida without an athletic code, I will have to add one more to my short list. Here are a few team rules to put on the radar.

My bus rule states that everyone rides the bus home from road games. Most athletic departments have parental travel forms so that parents can take their athlete home, but I feel it is important to be with the team in victory and defeat. On our road trips, we also collect cell phones, which is a captain responsibility and not officially a rule.

Attendance is an area that I struggled with early in my coaching career. My predecessor had a strict attendance policy. If you missed a practice for any reason, you missed a game. Our girls' season always overlapped with spring break, and if a player went on a family trip they suffered greatly once they returned. Our female athletes were afraid to go on school trips or family vacations. There were many complaints about that rule and it created tension with players and parents and hard feelings within the team.

Regarding practices, players are expected to be at every training session. If they cannot commit to attending practice every day they should re-evaluate their decision to join the team. If a practice is missed, the next player up is moved into the starting rotation, and when the absent player returns they have the opportunity to earn their spot back like everyone else. High school players will always have something come up. They are student-athletes, so if the player communicates about any after school make-up work or tutoring, they are not penalized. Communication is key when dealing with absences.

One season my athletic director received the infamous anonymous letter, this one stating that I was treating a player differently than the rest of the team regarding attendance. The player was playing significantly more time than the letter writer's son. He wanted to know why this player, who was late for practice three days a week, was allowed more time on the field than his son. The parent skipped our chain of command and went right to the athletic director.

The athletic director shared the letter with me while taking no action because it was my team and he was following our chain of command, however I still addressed the team. The player in question had some family issues that required his attention immediately after school almost every day. It was an issue the player told the team about and everyone was aware of the situation. We worked around it and the team did not have a problem with the arrangement. Obviously, one of our player's parents did, and between that player's lack of playing time and his family's frustration, the need to sound off in a letter was their answer.

We brought the issue up as a team once again, made sure everyone was on the same page, and moved on. I made it clear to the team that if they had a personal issue, communicating with me was a better option than an anonymous letter. The player eventually came and talked to me, apologizing for his father's actions. He was well aware of the team decision and had not shared the information with his parent. It was another example of a parent trying to fight their child's battles without knowing the full story. I remind parents every year to release their child to the team, to remember that the successes and failures belong to the athlete, and to let the student-athletes deal with any issues that arise.

In *Leading With the Heart* by Duke basketball coach Mike Krzyzewski, Coach K talks about rules and the need to keep it simple. I adopted that philosophy when I put my season handbook together. Our most important rule is to remember that you are always representing your family, your team, and yourself. In any decision you make, ask yourself if it is in your best interests. What effect will it have on your family, the team, and yourself? I give the team a little business card with positive comments on one side to help boost their self-esteem. On the flip side it states: "Don't do anything you wouldn't do in front of your mom."

26 SWEARING

What the @%#*!

Many coaches will disagree with me on this topic, but I do not allow the use of profanity on our practice field or in our games. This is not a rule, but an expectation, a standard of excellence. Once again referencing our core values, it falls under responsibility, respect, and integrity. This expectation is not only for the players in my program but for my staff as well. As a youth or high school coach, we should hold ourselves to a higher standard. If we do not want our athletes to swear, we have to set the example. Swearing in practice leads to swearing on the field and that behavior could cost you at some point during the season. The question for most coaches who want to curb the use of inappropriate language is how to police it.

I worked with a coach who used a yellow and red card system during training. If he heard a player swear he gave them a yellow card—a warning. If he heard the same player swear again, it was a red card and he would sit that player for one half of the next contest. During the two years I worked with that coach, I do not remember a player ever sitting out any amount of time for swearing. It was either a very effective tool, or the coach went deaf after issuing the yellow card. If a player did receive a yellow card and later dropped some language everyone could hear, was that coach really prepared to sit the player if the next game was of extreme importance?

Another coach would make a player run a lap around the field every time he heard them swear. To me that method disrupted the flow of practice and compromised the session. Regardless of the fact that I am not a fan of running for punishment anyway, I felt that it really had no positive outcome. Players would argue about swearing, jog around the field instead of run, and possibly create a negative or disruptive environment.

I have tried many different tactics to curb the use of inappropriate language throughout my tenure on the sideline. One season, I tried the running penalty, only I had my manager keep a tally if I identified the player, and then after the practice session the team would run sprints. By penalizing the team instead of just the violators, the team would then help police their teammates with the loose tongues. But as I stated, I am not a fan of running for punishment so I abandoned that practice.

The best solution I found is in the form of a team swear jar. Players that choose to let out an inappropriate word are fined. Swearing is absolutely not allowed, however we all know that kids will let one slip now and then—some players more than others. I put a 50-cent penalty on the F-bomb and all other words were a quarter. The manager kept a tally for me and all fines were due prior to the next contest. If the fine wasn't paid, the player would not take the field. The fines are not that severe unless the player has a serious problem with self-control.

One game, a player owed $7.50 and forgot to pay his fine. When he realized his error he ran around frantically, begging and borrowing to make his payment. I was prepared to sit him out but fortunately for him, his teammates came up with enough loose change.

I also imposed a five-dollar fine for any yellow or red cards for swearing or dissent in an actual contest, fines that were applied to the coaching staff as well. There was a game where my assistant failed to remember his role on the bench and received a bench yellow card for dissent. The team held him accountable and cheered as he pried a five-dollar bill out of his wallet at the next practice. At the end of the season, we use the money for a pizza party or make a charitable donation. We do have fun with it, too, at the end-of-season award banquet. The player accumulating the most fines is given a toilet brush and our Potty Mouth Award, something parents are always proud of.

If I have to police swearing, I prefer the financial system. All I have to do is record the incident during practice; it is not a disruption and the players seldom argue. When running was involved, denial was always an issue and practice would be paused. With the fines, there is seldom an argument and it is another reason to go out for a pizza.

27 THE OFF-SEASON

The off-season used to mean a break from soccer for the coach. Players would go off and play other sports or just be teenagers for a while. Then the season would roll around again and those players would dust off their boots and kick the ball around a little until it was time to start up again.

That was a simpler time. There are now numerous club opportunities, winter leagues, and indoor opportunities, as well as year-round tournament offerings. I have a t-shirt from a soccer convention that says "There is no off-season," and there truly isn't. We know that if our players are not touching the ball most of the year, our teams will be at a disadvantage. How do we provide these opportunities without demanding them? We try to instill in our players a love and passion for the game. If they are passionate about soccer, we will not have to demand anything of our players; they will seek out opportunities on their own.

I worked with a football coach who came in and turned around the high school football program. The staff he put together demanded weightlifting and conditioning throughout the off-season. If a player had a family vacation or a job with conflicting hours, they were told that off-season work came first. The coach had success when it came to wins and losses, but the sport became a job for these high school athletes. For some the demands of the program took away their passion for the game.

When the new soccer coach took over for me in Fond du Lac, he followed the lead of the football coaches and put a lot of pressure on his players to lift weights and attend other soccer activities. Many of the athletes participated in other sports as well and had to balance their soccer expectations with their other pursuits. Due to the extreme pressure that was put on the team to spend their entire off-season conditioning, eight seniors chose to do something else that fall. Coaches can offer activities and hope that players will take advantage of them, but they should also be aware of a player's need to work, go on a vacation, or focus on other pursuits. A little understanding and compassion can go a long way.

The off-season is a time for a player to pursue another sport, develop another passion, or continue to refine the game he or she loves. I offer off-season strength and conditioning, provide indoor soccer opportunities, open gyms, and help set up captains' practices. When players decide whether or not to participate in off-season improvement opportunities, they need to think about staying on the coach's radar. My players know that I follow their off-season pursuits and I will often attend their club games or their other high school sporting pursuits. They have many opportunities to fuel their own passion for the game; it is not my position to force or demand it of them.

The following is a twelve-month template of what I provide or is provided by the local club to help players feed their passion. High school soccer has many seasons: some play in spring, Florida plays in the late fall/winter, and my colleagues in Texas play a later winter season. You can use the fall guideline and adjust it to your own situation.

- **August**—Typically the season begins during the second week of the month. At one time, a high school preseason camp was offered by high school coaches who wanted to get a jump start on the season. The state associations took away that opportunity, so the alternative was that an outside group (a local college coach) held the camp. In Florida, it is illegal for any contact with your team in that two-week window. It is up to the players to make sure they are getting the rest they need or are playing on their own. If they are playing on a club team, they are still practicing and do not enjoy that break.
- **September and October**—This is the bulk of the fall season filled with practices and games.
- **November**—It's playoff time, and hopefully the team is still going in the early part of the month. At the conclusion of the season, my staff provides an open weight room for the players that want to lift. Club programs start up again and there are local indoor facilities that run winter leagues. Our players are encouraged to form their own teams and play for the fun of it and to feed their passion.
- **December**—Strength and conditioning opportunities continue and indoor leagues are abundant. Players are encouraged to pursue another high school sport or even to take a month off.
- **January and February**—Strength and conditioning is still offered and open gyms begin. We take advantage of open gym space and play futsal. Club programs are usually in full swing in Florida, so the players that are taking advantage of those opportunities are busy.
- **March, April, and May**—Strength and conditioning, futsal, and club opportunities continue.
- **June and July**—Strength and conditioning, open fields, and captains' practices are provided. Club programs are still in full swing. Strength and conditioning is promoted for those that are not

participating in anything else so they are prepared for the start of the season.

Summer is a great time to look for a team opportunity. There is a great high school tournament in Iowa every June in which teams register and have the opportunity to play five games in three days at a beautiful facility. We were able to put a package together and take 36 boys and girls to this event each summer. It was a fun, no-pressure tournament that also gave us a chance to get a look at the team we would put on the field that upcoming season.

Captains' practices are just that, practices run by the captains of the team. Usually the players agree on a time and place and just get together and play soccer with no coaches around. It is a great opportunity for your captains to organize and lead, and it puts the team in their hands.

With all of the off-season opportunities, communication is once again of extreme importance. Information must get to every player, and the coach needs to be as transparent as possible. If you have an opportunity that is limited to a smaller number, like our Iowa trip, it is important to identify how players will be selected.

My constant question to players is, "What have you done today to become a better soccer player?" Do your players know what it means to be on the coach's radar? Are you visible at their other events? Do you take an interest in them away from the game and outside of the season?

I had a junior varsity player from the previous season who was not a very big kid. He had some skill, but lacked the intensity and maturity that would be needed to earn a varsity spot. The player decided to run track that spring to work on his speed and endurance. He showed up at captains' practices and took advantage of the strength and conditioning program. This player pushed himself to improve in every area, staying on the radar. Not only did this young man make the varsity team, but he put himself in a position to challenge for a spot on the first eleven.

He surpassed other players that had much more athletic ability because he put forth more effort. For him, it was about working hard and staying on the radar screen. His drive and dedication did the rest.

The off-season is also a time for the coach to expand his or her own knowledge and stretch professionally. Familiarize yourself with the many coaching education programs that are available. My favorite courses have been the ones offered by the National Soccer Coaches Association of America (NSCAA). These courses focus on making you a better coach and are perfect for youth, high school, and college coaches.

Coaching, like life, is all about building relationships. The off-season is a time to interact with your players and continue to foster those positive relationships. Everyday while interacting with players, students, and people within our working environments, we have the opportunity to build relationships. I want my players, my staff, and the faculty I work with to want to play for me, to want to work with me, and to want to attend our games because we have built meaningful relationships. If you can build a meaningful relationship with each and every one of your players, it will be a season of significance, and that season extends to the so-called off-season.

28 PROMOTION

A very important, but often neglected, duty for a coach is the promotion of your team. None of us have the luxury of a press agent, a soccer beat reporter, or even a sports information department at our disposal. Often the local newspaper is understaffed and may have a limited amount of space allocated for high school sports. Expecting the newspaper to give your team great coverage is often unrealistic. That may mean you have to be the squeaky wheel when it comes to getting some press for your team. If you have the energy, here are a few things you can try.

With regards to the local newspaper and radio stations, I have found that the more you help them do their jobs, the more they'll be willing to help you promote your team. At the beginning of the season, we photograph head shots of all our varsity players and provide them to the local sports department. After each game, I write a brief synopsis of the contest with stats and descriptions of goals. I even throw in a quote from a player and then email that to my media contact list. If it is not too late, I follow that up with a call to the sports desk to see if they need anything else. If possible, I have a parent email an action shot from the game to the contact list as well. With much of their job being done for them, there is a greater chance they will print something.

The more I send and the more I contact them, the greater our relationship develops, leading to a higher likelihood that my players will get some local recognition. Radio stations will always report sports scores, so giving them statistics and quotes can give you added coverage as well. We developed such a good relationship with the local sports radio station that we eventually started to air two live games per season.

Parents can also be a big help when it comes to additional coverage. A nice letter or email to the sports department telling them about the team and the parents' interest in seeing more press can be helpful, especially if the parent has a business that advertises with that paper.

Promote your players and coaches whenever you get the opportunity. When one of my assistants, our JV coach, was named AFLAC Assistant Coach of the Year, we took a photo and sent a press release to the local newspaper and radio outlets. When our teams earned NSCAA academic recognition, we took a team photo and sent out a press release. Whenever a player was recognized for volunteer service or individual academic awards, we jumped on the opportunity to promote our players and our team. Despite the fact that our season is only three months long, we took every opportunity we could to keep soccer in the press throughout the year.

In 1999, I recognized that our community did not get very much soccer information in the media. Soccer had never been the most popular sport in our community. The old guard in the community neither understood nor appreciated the game. Soccer was often referenced as "a communist plot" by the elders at the local barbershop. I took it upon myself to try and infiltrate the media and push soccer to the front lines.

I went to the local paper and offered to write a weekly column titled, Just Dribblin' About, a 500-word piece about soccer each week—I guess it was a blog before blogs became a thing. Each week I wrote about the high school teams I coached, things going on with our local club, and the men's and women's national team. In the beginning, in order to get the article in the paper, I had to find a sponsor for my article. Not only did I have to write the article, I had to find businesses willing to pay $35 a week to sponsor it!

After the first year, the article attracted enough attention (both positive and negative) that I did not have to secure sponsorship anymore. It was a small victory and until I moved from that community, the residents received a dose of soccer each week whether they liked it or not. While I am not suggesting you take up a writing career, realize that sometimes you have to think outside the box to get your message to the masses.

There are countless promotional tools that you can use to get your team some publicity. Make a poster schedule with a team photo or a photo of your returning letter winners. Each season we would try and come up with a clever theme and do a photo shoot. For example, we had won two conference championships in a row and were looking to add a third. Our girls' team dressed in workout gear and we staged a photo in the weight room with the slogan "Pumped for a 3-Peat." Another year we chose "Beast Mode" as our theme and took a photo at a local outdoor retailer that had numerous pieces of stuffed wildlife. One year we went to a local mega-farm and had the team sit on a gigantic tractor with the slogan "Meet Us on the Field, It's Goin' Down!" Use your resources and your creativity.

These posters included the team schedule and sponsors as well as our team photo. We asked the players to solicit sponsorships to place on the poster. Each player attempted to find a $100 sponsor. The posters do not cost that much, so the additional money was used for team bonding activities.

We have also tried a "best seat in the house" promotion for our high school fans. Every high school student that attended the game received a ticket, and right before kick-off, a random ticket was drawn with the winner and a friend receiving the best seats in the house (i.e., a couch in the stands and a pizza from a local pizza business delivered to the winners in that seat).

We covered Teacher Appreciation Night in chapter 18, and you also have your standard Parents' Night, Senior Night, Junior High Night, or Youth Night. You went into coaching to work with athletes and use your passion for the game you love to influence young men and women. As you start working with these athletes, the need to see them recognized for the efforts they put in becomes important. Promoting them will start to take on more significance for you, and there are many ways to go about doing it.

As always, what you do in the area of promotion is only limited to your own creativity and energy level. If it is not your forte, then look for a parent or assistant that has a talent or desire to help you put a soccer assault on your community.

29 THE END-OF-YEAR BANQUET

There is no better way to cap off the season than with a postseason celebration. Banquets are the way to celebrate the work your players have put in and wrap up the season. I am not talking about meeting in the coach's classroom or the school cafeteria and sharing a few pizzas—I am talking about an event! Our banquets are held in a hotel banquet room with a nice dinner, or at a local restaurant that can accommodate our team.

The planning work on our postseason banquet is taken care of at the beginning of the season: the venue, the cost, and the date and time are provided at our initial parent meeting. We strongly encourage everyone to attend and to bring the entire family if they can. Our functions include a sit-down dinner, a PowerPoint presentation or highlight video, player introductions, and award presentations, and the evening is filled with stories about the season.

After we finish eating, the JV and freshman coaches give a brief synopsis of their season and pass out a few awards. Once they are finished, the varsity show begins. I usually schedule the event a month after the season is over because I spend a lot of time coming up with unique awards for every individual. Throughout the year I keep track of funny and embarrassing moments and I either buy or make a funny award to go along with the story. Every varsity player is brought up front and given their letter, certificate, or pin. Then a story is told and the award is handed out. Here are a few examples:

- During a game, I had a player almost climb up the back of one of his teammates to try and score a goal with his head. I drilled holes in a few 2x4s, and threaded rope through them to make a ladder that included loops at the end to go over a player's shoulders. I wrote a memory or individual statistic on each rung for the player at the banquet.
- Each year I get an oven mitt for the player with the most assists— The Helping Hand Award. I write our team name, the year, and the number of assists on the oven mitt.
- One of my players with a poor vertical jump scored a goal with her head after falling on the ground and then heading it while on her knees. I attached springs on the bottom of some old soccer cleats for her.
- Every player that scores a goal receives a Skor candy bar. Every player that logs 1,000 minutes receives a 100 Grand candy bar for reaching a grand in the minutes column.
- The season we survived the shooting at the hotel, and the shoot-out in our first game, each player received a t-shirt with the phrase "Bullet Proof" on the front. It was a tragic event, but a memory of how our team cared for each other.
- For the player that scores the most goals, I take an old cleat and screw it to a piece of 2x4 and spray paint it gold for the Golden Boot Award.
- The player who logs the most minutes receives the Iron Man Award. I can usually find an Iron Man figurine in a clearance rack somewhere.

- The player that has the hardest time controlling their mouth receives a toilet brush and toilet cleaner for the Potty Mouth Award.
- We had a player with numerous injuries, so I made a jacket out of bubble wrap for that player.

We have a lot of fun with our awards and often the parents leave with stomachaches from laughing so hard. We finish on a high note and everyone leaves excited about where we have been and ready to prepare for the next season.

Because there is an award for every player, each team member is recognized individually and a personal story is told. It re-affirms that each and every player is a significant and valued member of the team. It is a special evening for the player and their families and it makes the time it takes to come up with these awards and put them together extremely worthwhile.

Coaches and parents are not exempt from the awards either. I make sure there is a story about each coach when I introduce them, and if there is a parent that does something special for us, we recognize them with something nice as well as something funny. And of course I always make sure to recognize my wife! We had a parent host a pasta party for our team one year and she started a small fire in her kitchen, so she received a fireman costume. One father, who was very loud and could not keep his mouth shut, needed to be recognized as well. I took a hard hat, attached a mouthpiece, and then ran tubes from the mouthpiece to the ear holes so only he would be able to hear himself.

For me the banquet is a must. When I took over the Ida Baker boys' program they had never had a banquet. Most of the other programs had a banquet, but the previous coaches for soccer did not think it was important. When we held our first banquet the team and the parents were amazed and grateful. The banquet helped put some importance back into the soccer program.

Sometimes coaches are reluctant to do things that are out of their comfort zone. I had a colleague who was a varsity girls' basketball coach and he never wanted to have a banquet. The basketball boosters wanted to host a banquet and this coach would refuse. His reluctance affected the boys' program as well because what was done for one was done for the other. Finally the boys had a new coach who insisted on a banquet and the girls' coach finally agreed. He didn't talk much and just handed out the letters and plaques. Speaking in front of large groups was not his forte, but his lack of enthusiasm said something more than a fear of public speaking.

When I spoke with him about his reluctance to talk about his players he told me that he never knows what to say about the players on the end of the bench, the ones who do not play much. What it showed was that he was focusing on the starters and not spending as much time with the entire team. Ultimately, despite having very successful seasons, he was released from his coaching assignment. He was unable to create relationships with his players and their parents and was replaced.

If you are trying to create a season of significance for every player, relationships need to be cultivated with all of them. It should be easy to come up with a story about everyone because you have been a part of their lives for the past three to four months. Take the time to make your end-of-year banquet just as important as one of your contests. The memories from the banquet may last longer than any game played that season.

30 GAME OVER

The game is over, the victory is secured, the tough loss swallowed. Regardless of the outcome, we are on the bus and heading home. The ride is much like the process of putting four decades of coaching on paper. It is a time to reflect on what the team did well or what needs to be done at the next training session. During the ride, reflect on who came up big, who needs some positive reinforcements, and what worked for your team.

As I typed my ideas out on the keyboard it was interesting how many memories and relationships flooded back into my thoughts. I am reminded of a quote I read:

"One coach of significance impacts generations of athletes." –Proactive Coaching

We may never know the effect our coaching careers have on future generations. I have always put a priority on the relationships I have with my players. The wins and losses will eventually slip from our memories, but it is the relationships that will stand the test of time.

Each season I learn from my players and we challenge each other to be our best. Whether coaching youth, high school, or even beyond, players will remember the coaches who impacted their lives, the coaches who put a priority on making every season one of significance.

I am hoping as we ride this bus home together that you will be able to take things from this book and improve your coaching, your program, your ability to put character first, and your ability to make a significant impact on your players.

Good luck!

ACKNOWLEDGMENT

This book is a collection of stories and anecdotes that will help coaches as they guide their teams. For me, coaching has been and always will be a rewarding experience. I often learn as much from my teams as they learn from me, and most of it has nothing to do with the game itself. For me it will always be about the relationships that are built and grown on these journeys.

Thanks first of all to my family. Without the constant support of my wife Vikki, the coaching journey would have never been possible. Spending a lot of time with someone else's children is very demanding, and without the love and support of a spouse, this would not be a sustainable profession.

My four sons—Bart, Brett, Brock, and Brent—were also with me almost every step of this journey. Their participation on my teams was very rewarding and made it possible to develop deeper relationships with each of them. A special thank you to Brett as he provided his expertise and helped with the initial edit of the book.

My soccer journey began in Fond du Lac, Wisconsin. I want to thank the community for helping build one of the best youth soccer programs in the state in the 90s. There were many volunteers—both parents and former players—that helped us grow soccer in that community. The Fond du Lac School District and Fond du Lac High School allowed me to develop and grow my coaching career and I will be forever grateful for those opportunities.

I would also like to thank George Jenkins High School for providing the opportunity to bring my talents to Florida. New relationships are now being developed at Ida Baker High School on the west coast of Florida, bringing me new challenges and opportunities.

As you read this book, focus on how to build better relationships and foster team development. Examine what you really want to pass on to your players and why that is important. Coaching equals leading, and we can apply our leadership lessons in every aspect of our lives.

Keep on kickin'!

CREDITS

Cover design: Claudia Sakyi

Layout and Typesetting: Katerina Georgieva

Photos: © Vikki Winkler

Graphics: © Thinkstock
           © Greg Winkler (p. 19)
           Florida SouthWestern Collegiate (p. 20)

Copyediting: Anne Rumery

THE BEST TRAINING REGIMES FOR YOUR TEAM

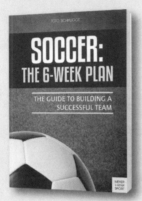

Toto Schmugge

SOCCER: THE 6-WEEK PLAN

THE GUIDE TO BUILDING

A SUCCESSFUL TEAM

Toto Schmugge has created the perfect 6-week plan to help coaches of any skill and experience level to give their team a competitive edge and gain confidence as a coach. With these exercises, any player will learn techniques and tactics and improve their strength, speed, endurance, and agility. The exercises are described in detail and very easy to follow. Illustrations for every exercise provide the coach with visual aids to explain the drill.

232 p., in color,
54 photos + 150 illus.,
Paperback, 6 1/2" x 9 1/4"

ISBN: 9781782550921

$ 16.95 US/$ 26.95 AUS
£ 11.95 UK/€ 15.95

HOW THE BEST WIN
AND CAN BE BEATEN

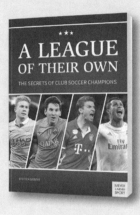

A ENTERTAINING

HISTORY OF SOCCER

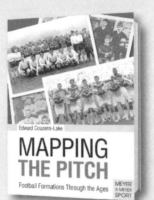

Edward Couzens-Lake

MAPPING THE PITCH

FOOTBALL FORMATIONS

THROUGH THE AGES

This book is an entertaining exploration of the history and evolution of football formations from the Victorian age to the 2014 World Cup in Brazil. The author analyses the thinking behind the popular formations and shows how the thinking behind the game changed in football from the late 19th century onwards.

304 p., b/w,
31 photos, 13 illus.,
Paperback, 5 3/4" x 8 1/4"

ISBN: 9781782550600

$ 14.95 US/$ 22.95 AUS
£ 9.95 UK/€ 14.95

MEYER & MEYER Sport
Von-Coels-Str. 390
52080 Aachen
Germany

Phone   +49 02 41 - 9 58 10 - 13
Fax   +49 02 41 - 9 58 10 - 10
E-Mail   sales@m-m-sports.com
Website   www.m-m-sports.com

All books available as e-books.

MEYER
& MEYER
SPORT